Learning and Teaching
in the
Elementary School

by

PHILIP D. VAIRO

and

ROBERT J. KRAJEWSKI

The Scarecrow Press, Inc.

Metuchen, N. J.   1974

Library of Congress Cataloging in Publication Data

Vairo, Philip D   comp.
    Learning and teaching in the elementary school.

    CONTENTS: Shuman, R. B. Citykid.--Bazeli, F. P.
Some practical advice on teaching children in the inner
city.--Krajewski, R. J. Technological aides: implications for inner-city teaching strategies. [etc.]
    1. Education, Elementary--United States--Addresses,
essays, lectures. 2. Education, Urban--United States--
Addresses, essays, lectures. I. Krajewski, Robert J.,
joint comp. II. Title.
LB1569.V34   372.1'1'02   74-8706
ISBN 0-8108-0764-5

To

Lillian and Lynn

CONTENTS

CITYKID

R. Baird Shuman

They took the boy out of the city
But no matter how they tried
They could not wrest the city magic
From the boy.

He looked at trees and rushing streams
And in them saw reminders of light posts
And teams of people flooding into subway stops
At half past five.

They told him he must walk in woods through autumn gold,
That he must learn to hunt and fish to be a man
But he had hunted, fished for coins through gratings
And walked in autumn moods at ten or twelve
When people prowl the streets to make seductions,
When eyes peer in the darkness avidly like Rousseau's
        tigers
And hands stroke body parts bound tight in clothes.

The boy was made to feel he was wrong
And they were right.
For, with them, there was no middle ground,
Just right and those who did not fit its mold:
The boy, enduring now in their good hands
The punishment, the soul starvation
Of a rehabilitation
Out of town.

R. Baird Shuman, "Citykid," English Journal (May 1968),
p. 679. Reprinted with the permission of NCTE and the
author.

1. SOME PRACTICAL ADVICE ON TEACHING CHILDREN IN THE INNER CITY

Frank P. Bazeli

All right! So you know about the background of your inner city children; you're aware of their needs, motivations, concerns and interests; you've suffered through what you think were Mickey Mouse education courses; and you try to keep abreast of the latest writing in the field of compensatory education. But you have classrooms full of children and each one is different. You don't have research consultants hovering about; you don't have fantastic quantities of supplies and equipment; you don't have paraprofessionals to help out. You just have kids you want to teach. Some learn as well as any suburban kid; most don't. What can you do?

Background

First, go back to the theorists. Read Jerome Bruner's Toward a Theory of Instruction, B. F. Skinner's The Technology of Teaching, and writings about Piaget's theories of intellectual development. This time, however, take the experiments described in these books and try them out on your students. This will turn you into a researcher rather than a pattern follower. Incidentally, you will find out many fascinating and useful things about what your children can do and to what degree.

Study the cumulative folders kept on your children. Be thorough. Take notes on everything you can glean from the records which will help you in working with each child.

Frank P. Bazeli, "Some Practical Advice on Teaching Children in the Inner City," The Clearing House (November 1972), pp. 170-172. Reprinted by permission of the author and publisher.

Some popular writers in education take the position that test
results and other evaluative information are pernicious, in
that they influence teachers' attitudes toward children.   If
your attitude about a pupil switches from positive to negative
on the basis of what you read in his folder, get out of
teaching.

        Advising educators to ignore educational data on
children is like asking physicians to ignore a patient's
medical test results and his medical history.   While you
can carry the analogy too far, without information diagnosis
and prescription are ineffective. It is presumed that you are
well aware of the limitations of standardized measurements
of inner city children.   Their environments provide experiences which are substantially different from those assumed
to be common by test makers preparing instruments for
national norms.   Now that you are reminded, if you needed
to be, use the data in a professionally critical manner.

Content

        Review the content of your courses.   For some of
you this will be a revealing exercise if you ask the following
questions: Of what real use is this to my pupils?   Whose
interests are served by using this material?   Does the content include special topics designed specifically for my kids?
The chances are that most of you have been following a run-
of-the-mill, standard program based on what some university professor thinks people ought to know about his discipline.   Be hard nosed.   You should be selecting from a
discipline materials and content you and the children find
useful and interesting.   Create and shape your own courses
to your own specifications.   To do it any other way means
that you're not a professional; you're a skilled worker.

        You keep hearing about instructional and performance
objectives in education.   Chances are that most of you are
not sure what they mean.   Although it seems simple enough,
devising instructional objectives can be frustrating.   Read
Robert Gagne's The Conditions of Learning, Bloom's Taxonomy of Educational Objectives, and Robert Mager's Preparing Instructional Objectives.   Using these as guides, devise a set of educational objectives for your courses.   Get
the kids to help in the formulation of these goals.   Upon
reflection you will begin to see what content, materials,
and experiences will be necessary to allow the pupils to

achieve some degree of mastery over the objectives.

The inability to achieve mastery over a complex
skill or to understand and use a set of concepts or principles is usually the result of not having learned sub-skills
and lower order verbal associations which support an understanding of the higher level learning. When children are
bewildered, examine what they would need to know to be
able to grapple with the problem. It is usually the case that
you've tried to work at too high a level. If the instructional objectives have been carefully devised, they'll look like
pyramids or hierarchies of understandings leading up to complex generalizations. For instance, just for a moment, consider what a five-year-old would need to know in order to fit
together a puzzle. Now consider what you assume a sixteen-
year-old is able to do when you ask him to write a short story.
If neither learner is able to accomplish his task, the reason
can probably be found with careful analysis.

Methods

Now that you have sensible courses, tailored to the
needs of your students with well-defined objectives, ranging
from simple stimulus-response type learning to complex
generalizations, how do you arrange the day-to-day classroom activities to reach these objectives? Educational
psychologists have many suggestions; the most prominent
have turned into slogans which can be parroted and then
ignored. This is especially true in ghetto schools where
teachers typically are suffering from tunnel vision with
nearly all their energies directed toward keeping control
over the class. Very often the technique that keeps the
children in their seats and relatively quiet is at least safe
if not particularly effective. That's not good enough.

Because most of them can't read very well and have
a tough time conceptualizing, pupils want the security of
workbook type seat work and concrete, example-filled opera-
tions. They enjoy discussions, where they can express
opinions about events and situations of which they have first-
hand knowledge, but question-answer sessions on abstract
principles frustrate them if they have not been well grounded.
Therefore, during the first part of the year emphasize low
order learning, such as signal learning, simple S-R bonds,
chaining and sequencing of stimulus-response bonds, verbal
associations, and multiple discriminations. Read Gagne's

writings for an extensive description of these learnings.

In building the base of sub-skills and information use operant conditioning devices such as programmed material and workbook type lessons. Describe and explain each step in the task very carefully. Use pictures, filmstrips, drawings, cartoons, films, and TV programs to back up your explanations. Spend a lot of time clarifying and defining the works and symbols they need to know.

Now this is important: Have the pupils explain each step back to you or to each other as they run through the process. This method is called teach-teach back, if you're interested. What is important is the verbalization of the activity so that concepts and principles can be mentally manipulated later in the course.

During these first weeks plan an individual program for each child based on his test records and special needs and interests. Each day have him spend a part of class time on his own program. That sounds threatening and time-consuming, but while you'll work hard initially this preparation will make you much more efficient. You'll end up with more free time later, simply because the kids will be working individually much of the time. Keep goal cards or an open record book in which your pupils can record and chart their progress. During each class period make sure that you talk to and evaluate the work of every child. One minute of personal attention produces surprising results.

In describing a concept or principle, first show what it is and what it is not, where it is applied and how it works. Use at least two methods of explanation and demonstration. Use audio-visual effects because inner city kids like to see how things operate. After this is done, have the kids work with it in simulated experiences, verbalizing the application as they use it. Later, the higher order learning should be integrated with others and their transfer abilities to life situations demonstrated. If they don't see any use in what they learn, they'll just forget it.

Motivation

Much of the time, your pupils won't be convinced that their interests are served by what you're trying to teach them. Also, having failed too often, they're programmed to fail. Do away with failure as a motivational device; substitute success and reward. Look into the writings on behavior modification, such as Bandura's <u>Principles of Behavior Modification</u> for ideas. Extrinsic rewards (such as tokens with which pupils can buy free time or their way into a dance) for work done might pain your sense of values, but ghetto kids know reality another way. Combined with obvious progress visually portrayed on charts, graphs, and goal cards, which support a sense of success when they know what the teacher is talking about, extrinsic rewards add to their motivation. They have a little action to make things interesting.

These suggestions probably sound very strange to you if you've been in the habit of moving from page to page in some textbook until you arrive at the end of the semester or the end of the book, whichever comes first. If you follow a program or a pattern without a critical understanding of what it's all about, you can be replaced by a more efficient machine.

If you're a pro, I haven't told you a thing you don't know.

2. TECHNOLOGICAL AIDES: IMPLICATIONS FOR INNER-CITY TEACHING STRATEGIES

Robert J. Krajewski

Some teachers would say, under present teaching arrangements, that individualization of instruction can never be more than a dream. In most elementary schools, classes are neither homogeneous nor small enough, and teachers are unable to adjust adequately for individual differences. Every learner is handicapped in some way--the fast, being held down by the pace of the slower, with boredom, frustration and loss of powers not sufficiently exercised; and the slow, never quite mastering a skill, yet always pressured to move on to the next objective. Utilizing technology, the teacher can better assure the fast learner's moving ahead at a pace adjusted to his rate of learning and the slow learner's knowing each lesson before he is permitted to move forward, thus eliminating those perpetual frustrations which serve as obstacles to educational achievement.

Inner-city children come to school with a wealth of knowledge, a vast background acquired from simply existing in their city environment. These children have been exposed to many sights and sounds; they have experienced much in their short lives. Unfortunately, the experiences and knowledge thus attained are not always of the kind most desired by teachers in the urban schools. Too often these children are just looked upon as being disadvantaged--why not, since that's the simplest way out. Actually, however, when compared to their suburban counterparts, some or most of these children may in fact be advantaged in many respects. We, as educators, can not and must not simply categorize these children as disadvantaged. They, as other children, come to school with varying degrees of abilities, experiences, deprivations, achievements and learning styles. Some may learn more easily by seeing, some by hearing, some by touching, and

Unpublished paper, included by permission of the author.

some by doing. Having been brought up and primarily educated by city life and the "Big Daddy, " television, the inner-
city youngsters are accustomed to fast action and large doses
of creativity. How dull it must be for them to enter the
classroom at the age of five or six, be seated behind desks,
face a chalkboard and be expected to learn now with paper,
pencils and books.

Urban administrators and teachers are primarily
responsible for establishing classrooms to provide the kind
of education inner-city children require.   They are the ones
who must work and plan together to implement change.   They
must constantly seek new methods of approach to involve
children in satisfactorily reaching higher goals in education.

The teacher in the urban classroom must first accept
the children, taking into account the different rates of growth,
styles of learning and problems of adjustment to school.
The urban child, as any other school age child, should feel
secure in his surroundings and in what he is doing. Frequent, immediate and positive feedback stimulates him to do
his work and progress in a sequential manner at his level
of ability. It gives him a self-satisfying feeling of success.
This in turn provides him with good feelings about himself.
He becomes more involved, begins to establish goals (minor
ones at first) and then strives toward achieving them.
Attention and individual treatment by concerned teachers is
a must for every inner-city child.

The instructional program offered to inner-city children should include vast amounts of student participation.
Materials utilized must provide for frequent repetition, often
in varying formats. Rewards for work must occur frequently.
By providing individualized instruction, the teacher can work
with each urban child at his own level and pace, and make
the child's activities relevant to his interests, learning styles
and goals. Through the use of individualized instruction the
teacher is more assured of each child mastering the skills
and utilizing them in workable fashion.

Historically, scholastic or formal education has been
achieved through the guidance of a teacher. This guidance
role has not changed; however, means now available to teachers for presenting information have drastically changed.
Formerly, but not too far past, the teacher had little more
than his voice, the chalkboard, and the textbook to convey
the message of his discipline. Today, however, a plethora

of instructional materials is available for classroom use, and
there is growing teacher awareness of how to incorporate
these materials into their teaching. Education for the urban
child must come alive!

It is impossible for one teacher to reach every child
in today's crowded inner-city classrooms and to provide for
each child the exact curriculum needed. The teacher must
have helpers. But wait, need they be additional teachers or
aides? No, not necessarily, for technological aides of all
types can be utilized most successfully in helping teachers
to reach the individual child.

Technological aides, in many forms, can help make
instruction more stimulating, exciting, and meaningful. In
appealing to various senses, they can be used at any time,
on any level, and at any rate desired. In addition, they
allow for either group or individualized instruction to become
a vital part of the instructional program. Technological aides
will give the teacher a more realistic approach in presenting
and implementing his lessons. Learning can then take place
through affective associations. For example, a person may
think he knows many meanings of a word because he has read
definitions or has a small amount of experience. In actuality
he may have an incomplete and vague understanding of these
meanings. Does he know, for example, what an ostrich is
really like until he sees one at the zoo or sees a motion picture scene of herds of them in Australia? Could he actually
know the magnificent sight of the ocean unless he had been
there or had seen it on film? This is the function of audio-
visual materials; to provide experience, more or less direct,
whereby a student can learn through visual and/or audio
associations. Learning then becomes more meaningful.

In contrast to the symbolic nature of words, audio-
visual materials are much more like real-life experiences.
Through the technological aides, presentation of facts is more
easily and correctly absorbed. Consequently, the direct
appeal, by producing strong interest and clear meaning, increases the retention of what has been learned. What a great
way for each teacher to promote the use of individualized instruction. The daily activities of the teacher change from
lecture to more emphasis on diagnosis of pupils' strengths
and weaknesses, prescription of instructional tasks, and individual assistance to students. Now, as pupils work and progress at their own rates and levels, the teacher can spend
more time reinforcing individual students as they begin to

master the skills.

At this point, let us focus attention on several technological aides available to the teacher in the inner-city classroom.

Perhaps one of the first mechanical audiovisual items
to be widely used in the classroom was the motion-picture
projector. The motion and sound film allows reality of many
subjects to become a living part of the classroom. Through
the use of films a whole new world can be placed before the
students' eyes in a short time. The students can be shown
things that could rarely if ever be physically brought into the
classroom. This gives the student a much closer relationship with the referent than could be possible with a diagram
and verbal description. Like any teaching exercise, the
success will be determined by the teaching quality of the film.
The teacher, therefore, has a responsibility to choose films
carefully, with definite teaching goals in mind. He should
preview the film, prepare the students for the lesson, and
then conclude with a follow-up lesson.

Closely akin to the audible motion picture projector is
the filmstrip projector. Many of these are operated without
the benefit of sound; however, written information is on each
frame. This information can be read orally by either the
teacher or students. Some of the more recent models are
equipped with either records or tapes synchronized to give
explanations or comments as the pictures are shown. The
sound models can be used in the same way as the motion
picture projector, the difference being that the filmstrip cannot give the effect of motion.

The slide projector can also be used to bring reality
and interest into the classroom. The students are not left
to form mental images on their own from the spoken word,
but can actually view the concept to further guide their understanding. Although the slide projector is most frequently
used without the combination of sound, it can be synchronized
with sound, thereby bringing another dimension to its useful-
ness.

When considering using either the filmstrip or slide
projector, it is worth noting that the filmstrip projector is
generally limited to use with commercially prepared programs;
with the slide projector, the teacher may easily use slides of
his own creation.

Within the past few years another sound and motion picture aide has been brought to the classroom in the form of special programming made available by educational television stations. The television set which entertained and educated the preschool child at home is being utilized to better reach the student academically in the classroom. Many such programs are geared especially toward the inner-city child. They are creative, imaginative, witty, stimulating, educational, and make many children eager to watch and participate from the sidelines. An aide in learning?--by all means! Educational television allows the students of many different classrooms to receive instruction from one expert teacher, all at the same time. It should go without saying that this makes for excellent utilization of the exceptional teacher's talents. By using work sheets and related materials obtained from the television studio, the classroom teacher can make the programs a regular portion of the class curriculum.

The strategy of teaching by television is actually still in its infancy. The coming years will undoubtedly bring more and more educationally programmed curricula into the classrooms by way of the television set.

Besides the programming available from educational networks, many institutions are making their own programs for classroom use by utilizing closed-circuit television. These facilities use video-tape equipment to record a presentation for future use. This, like the educational network productions, allows for maximum exposure of a teacher and teaching techniques to more students than could otherwise be reached. Here again, by using work sheets and related materials, the video-taped programs can be integrated into the curriculum.

The use of television in the classroom can have its problems. A problem common to both network and closed-circuit television is the inability of a student to ask questions and to have discussions directly with the television instructor. Again, the guidance role of the classroom teacher becomes most important. The use of television programs does not mean that the classroom teacher can relax. He, too, must be involved for the program to be of full benefit to his students. He must prepare his students for the lesson (most educational television series issue informational background and suggestions pertaining to their lessons) and then follow the lesson up so that it does not become an isolated experience with no further relationships.

Two items of audio equipment which lend themselves
well to classroom use are the record player and the tape
recorder. The record player is a seasoned veteran in the
classroom whose varied uses include: mood-setting music
for creative art, drama, dancing, and writing; programmed
instruction for most any discipline (especially reading);
story telling; happy listening, and much more. In short, the
record player is limited only to the difficulty of finding
appropriate materials to fulfill the needs of students.

The tape recorder, a tremendous second teacher, has
only the limitation of the teacher's imagination in finding ways
to use it. The tape recorder provides all the pre-program-
med advantages of the record player plus the added advantage
of being able to let the children express themselves, to read
into the machine and then actually hear what they have produced. It becomes a learning aid to the individual child as
he excitedly hears the playback of his own voice. Both the
record player and the tape recorder have excellent potential
for use in individualized instruction through audio-centers.
The audio-centers allow one child or as many as eighteen
to listen at once without disturbing other members of the
class. This type of activity allows the teacher to work with
more than one child or group in different sections of the
same room, thus permitting more opportunity for individual
children to work on skills and levels matching their abilities.

Another seasoned veteran of the classroom is the overhead projector, which allows material to be projected on a
screen rather than having to be written on the chalkboard.
Color transparencies, either commercially or teacher/stu-
dent-prepared, can provide enlarged diagrams and written
ideas for easier viewing. Overlays might be used to approach difficult concepts in a step-by-step fashion. One
major consideration is that in contrast to the chalkboard,
teacher/student eye contact is maintained at all times. In
addition, the overhead projector can be used under normal
classroom lighting conditions.

The opaque projector is used in approximately the
same way as the overhead, the difference being, as the name
implies, that the opaque projector projects opaque materials
rather than transparencies on the screen. It is used primarily to project materials from books, art works, small
objects, etc. for the entire class to view. One disadvantage
of the opaque projector is that the teacher is unable to write
or draw illustrations on the material at the same time that it

is being viewed. Room lights must normally be extinguished during the opaque projector's use.

The Hoffman Reading Machine, the Language Master, the Cycloteacher, Systems 80 and other such reading machines provide the teacher additional methods of individualizing teaching within the classroom.

Generally, in the use of all technological media the teacher plays the important role. The teacher aides are, as stated, simply aides. The teachers should use them rather than letting them use the teachers. All materials utilized in fulfilling the needs of students must have relevance; they must be selected and previewed with basic goals in mind. Things like color, sound, scenes, and information must be up to date. Further, the teacher must make students aware of basic objectives both of content and manner of presentation. After each experience, the teacher should involve students in a follow-up plan of some type to further reinforce their learning.

Some people feel that the use of technological aides will dehumanize teaching. Not so; in fact, it may very well have the reverse effect, since the teacher will have more planning time to prepare for individual students and more opportunity to interact with his students. How important this is, especially when the inner-city child is involved--he wants a good education and we must provide him with it; he must have all the advantages that education can provide on an individual basis. The teacher cannot fulfill all his needs as a one-man team, but with the combination and adequate use of technological tools he is well on his way to providing for the inner-city child an educational program to meet his needs.

3. ORAL READING IN THE URBAN ELEMENTARY SCHOOL

Ruth A. Korey

Oral reading has certain benefits for all children, especially those who are disadvantaged. It also presents serious problems, especially for the disadvantaged. The round-robin method, each child reading aloud in turn, does more harm than good. Hoetker[1] has characterized such reading as "an excruciating and embarrassing experience for all concerned." On the other hand, there are very real benefits to be derived from reading aloud in choral reading and in dramatics.

This chapter includes a short history of oral reading, testing reading achievement by means of oral tests, problems in oral reading, procedures for choral reading, a section on dramatics, and a discussion of reading aloud by the teacher.

History of Oral Reading

In the past, generations of children went to school knowing that round-robin reading would be an inevitable part of each day's routine. They valiantly tried to "keep the place," while the teacher called on the pupils in the order of their seating and carefully corrected all mistakes in decoding. For these children, although they could not put the idea in words, reading and decoding were synonymous.

Some children learned to read by this method. Others had to repeat several grades and dropped out before completing the eight years of elementary school.

Eventually, educators realized that there is more to reading than decoding, that meticulous correction of one pupil's errors does not instruct other members of the class,

---

Unpublished paper, included by permission of the author.

and that children do not read along with the pupil who has
been called on.   Instead, they try to avoid the embarrass-
ment of not "knowing the place" when their turn comes.   It
was also realized by educators that oral reading is a more
complex mental activity than silent reading, and that it should
therefore be a final rather than an initial activity in the
reading of a textbook passage or story.

It should be remembered that oral reading is especially difficult for the urban child who speaks Black English,
Spanish, or another language at home.   Not only must he
decode words and sentences presented in standard English,
but in order to understand what he decodes he must translate it in his mind into his native language, and then back
into standard English for oral rendition.

With this realization, oral reading then took a minor
role.   Following Betts' classic formula[2] for basal reading
instruction, the teacher set up a background for the story,
taught the new words, and guided the children with questions
as they read silently.   Only after these activities were the
pupils asked to select and read aloud short passages in
answer to such questions as "What part showed that John was
brave?"; "What part did you consider funny?"; "What part
did you like best?"

This procedure provides two of the prerequisites for
successful oral reading--familiarity with the material on the
part of the child who reads aloud, and an audience situation
where the pupils have reason to listen to each other's oral
rendition.

Beginning teachers were sent out to their classes with
a set of rules regarding oral reading:

1.   Never use the round-robin method.

2.   Never ask a child to read aloud material that
     he has not previously read silently.

3.   Create an audience situation in which the
     pupils will want to listen to each other be-
     cause the material is new, or because it is
     approached from a new viewpoint.

These three commandments, coupled with Betts' formula and
varied language activities, gave even beginning teachers a

chance to instruct their pupils successfully in reading.

There are, of course, some exceptions to these rules.
First-grade and also mentally-retarded children need to
speak the words in order to grasp the first fundamentals of
reading. Needless to say, the pupils should take turns in
some manner other than round-robin order.

Testing with Oral Reading

Another exception for unprepared oral reading is the
preliminary screening which the teacher gives at the beginning of the school year. Over a period of four or five days,
each pupil reads without preparation one sentence from the
grade basal reader. The pupils at one table, or in one row,
are asked to read one sentence aloud from the basal reader.
From this simple procedure, the teacher can estimate the
reading achievement of each child--whether he is on grade
level or in need of further testing. In this case, the children
can be called on in rapid succession, with the teacher saying
"Next!" each time, as in the round-robin or "barber-shop"
days.

The Gilmore Oral Reading Test[3] and the Gray Oral
Reading Test[4] are useful for individual diagnosis. The Gilmore Oral Reading Test, which contains passages of increasing difficulty, includes such items as substitutions, mispronunciations, insertions, hesitations, repetitions, omissions,
and disregard of punctuation. It also brings to the teacher's
attention symptoms such as word-calling, monotone, high-
pitched voice, overloudness, oversoftness, and poor enunciation.

The Gray Oral Reading Test, which has four forms,
each containing thirteen passages of graded difficulty, provides insights into the level of sight reading, the ability to
decipher unfamiliar words, the number and types of error in
relation to speed of reading, and comprehension of literal
meaning.

Problems in Oral Reading

The items focused on in the oral reading tests are
symptomatic of deeper trouble--physical, emotional, or
pedagogic.

A physical checkup is essential.   Malnutrition, insufficient rest or exercise, poor eyesight or defective hearing
are often found in urban children because of the parents'
lack of money and lack of knowledge as to where to go for
help.

Emotional problems can be evidenced by extreme
restlessness or apathy in class, anxiety or shyness, aggres-
siveness and disruptive behavior.   These are signals for
referral to the school psychologist or guidance worker.
Waiting lists for these services are usually long. In the
meanwhile, and all during the period of therapy, the teacher
should do everything possible to help the child become a
good reader.   We do not know whether reading failure causes
or is caused by emotional problems, but we do recognize that
reading success will increase self-confidence, thus tending to
ameliorate other emotional problems which exist.

Difficulties in oral reading may be academic in origin.
The child may have missed important parts of beginning reading instruction through frequent or prolonged absence, or
through being taught by a method which uses analysis exces-
sively and does not provide for sufficient whole-word recognition.

The most common symptom of poor reading achievement is "word-calling," a term which applies to reading
aloud word by word instead of in logical phrases.   Focusing
instruction on this aspect of oral reading will contribute to
the child's general progress.   Several authorities in reading
instruction have written on the subject of word-calling, including Dolch, Betts, and Harris.

Dolch[5] has recommended intensive study of commonly
used phrases containing commonly used words.   He urged
drill on phrase cards incorporating his 95 commonly occurring
nouns and 220 basic sight words.   Dolch has classified such
phrases under the following headings: short sentences, pro-
noun and verb, modified subject, intransitive verbs, and
dependent clauses.   He believed that some transfer of training
does exist--that from the study of phrase material the child
may develop a mind-set toward larger units than the word.
He will then try to "read words together," consciously or
unconsciously, and will try to cover an area, rather than a
word, with his eyes.

In Foundations of Reading Instruction, Betts[6] stated

that a well-modulated voice is possible when oral reading has
been preceded by silent reading and when problems of word
recognition and comprehension in the material have been
cleared away. He believed that word by word reading and
the use of a high-pitched, strained voice are symptoms of
frustration induced by inability to deal with the reading material. The remedy is a lower level of difficulty. There is
no use in insisting on a conversational tone when the material
is too advanced for the child.

A second cause of word-calling, according to Betts,
is lack of adequate silent reading preparation. If the child
has no difficulty in silent reading, but still is unable to do
satisfactory oral reading, additional silent reading preparation may be required.

A third case, as viewed by Betts, may be the emotional
situation. Insecurity in the oral reading situation may be related to a speech defect, an unfavorable audience, or lack of
motivation. In such cases help for the speech defects should
be sought if needed. The teacher is the key to developing a
better audience situation and more effective motivation for
reading.

In How to Increase Reading Ability, Harris[7] has identified two types of word-callers: first, those who have difficulty in recognizing the words, and second, those who have a
habit of paying attention to only one word at a time.

In the first instance, the child needs thorough training
in word recognition, with mastery of a basic sight vocabulary
and of essential skills for unlocking unfamiliar words. As
speed of recognition and confidence develop, the word-calling
problem will gradually diminish.

Harris[8] has suggested the following devices to help
the child perceive phrases and think of reading as a grouping
of words.

1. Flash cards using phrases.

2. Games of following directions, such as "Close
the door," printed on the chalkboard.

3. Assembling groups of word cards into sentences,
either at desk or in wall pocket chart.

4. Workbook type exercises requiring the child to underline phrases or choose the answer to a question from a group of phrases, e.g., "Where did they get the wood?
   In the garden
   From the grocery
   At the lumber yard."

5. Workbook exercises consisting of two similar columns of phrases in different order, for the child to match.

6. Mimeographed material requiring the child to mark with slash lines the divisions between thought units, or draw curved lines under words which constitute a unit.

7. Material typed by the teacher for reading aloud, with large spaces between thought units, e.g., "The boy   is going   to the store   for some milk."

8. Thorough teaching of the meaning and purpose of capitalization and punctuation marks, especially the period and comma. Mimeographed, already punctuated material can be marked with crayons by the pupils as follows: red (stop) for periods, yellow (caution) for commas, and green (go ahead) for capital letters. Later on, unpunctuated mimeographed passages may be distributed for the pupils to insert capitals and punctuation independently as they read aloud. (This latter step presupposes that the children have had time to read the passage silently.)

9. Questions asked by the teacher beginning with who, what, where, when, how and why, to call attention to the meaning of simple and, later, more difficult sentences.

10. Commercial or homemade tachistoscopes, projection flash meters, or a homemade device in which reading material is seen through a slit in a cardboard which is moved across the page.

Harris has given two cautions to the teacher who is trying to improve pupils' oral reading: first, plan for needed carryover from exercise material to general reading; and second, don't expect the pupils to see too much at one fixation, as even college students need several fixations per line of type.

Another practice which deserves attention is the use of prosodynic print--letting all the children read together, noting the large print for loud passages, small print for softer rendition, small spaces between words to indicate short pauses, and wider spaces to denote longer pauses. This technique has been used successfully by Cukras[9] with middle class pupils. Experimental use of simple prosody with urban children should be explored as an aid to meaningful reading.

Choral Reading

Reading in concert, as in choral reading, poses no threat to the slow pupil such as he feels when individual members of the class are called on to read aloud. He may look forward to the time of choral reading as the one activity where he feels "safe." He will learn some reading skills incidentally at such a time.

Finger plays in kindergarten and first grade serve as an introduction to group reading, an activity which seems to please all children and is particularly valuable for the disadvantaged. One of the best collections for this purpose is Rhymes for Fingers and Flannelboards, by Scott and Thompson.[10] Many of the verses tend to strengthen numerical concepts as well as develop reading readiness skills--especially the understanding of word families through frequent exposure to rhyming words.

Another preliminary to choral reading is the language-experience chart. Here the children dictate the class chart following a trip, a party, or an interview with one of the school personnel. The teacher reads the chart back to the class and then suggests that the class as a whole read it back to her. If the charts are based on real experiences suitable for older children, this practice can be continued with slow readers throughout the elementary grades.

For choral reading itself, the teacher may select a poem from a book such as Time for Poetry,[11] edited by Arbuthnot and Root. This collection contains a long section

for the teacher, with a good explanation of verse choirs.   A
verse choir is the speaking counterpart of a glee club, with
pupils classified according to type of voice, intensive training,
meticulous leadership by teacher or choirmaster, and eventual
performance before an audience.   A skillful and well-trained
verse choir can produce entertaining and dramatic effects of
true theatrical quality.   It may be used occasionally in an
upper grade which has had long and successful practice with
choral reading.

Choral reading differs from the verse choir in that it
is informal and experimental, done for the pleasure of the
participants and with no thought of preparing for an audience.
This is the type of oral reading experience that urban children
need.

The method of introducing a choral reading selection
to a class is somewhat similar to the initial steps in a basal
reader lesson.   The teacher helps the children to establish
background understandings, clarifies difficult words, and then
reads the poem or prose selection several times to the class.
Children are encouraged to join in on any lines they remember,
especially on the refrain if there is one.

The pupils must be able to see the selection and read
along with the teacher.   Mimeographed copies may be distributed, or a large copy on chart paper may be used.

A brief discussion follows, with such questions as:
"What is the mood of the poem?"; "How does it make you
feel?"; "Should it be read quickly or at a slower pace?";
"Should the reading be smooth or staccato?"; "Which lines
should be loud?"; "Which lines should be soft?"

Various forms of organization may be used, depending
on the experience and reading skill of the class.   If most of
the pupils are hesitant oral readers, the teacher can read
the body of the selection, with the whole class reciting the
refrain.   This can be done with such prose as Chicken Little
or Rumpelstiltskin, as well as with poetry.

If there are questions and answers in the selection,
the questions may be asked by the boys and answered by the
girls, or vice versa.   Or half the class (on the basis of
seating) may ask the questions and the other half read the
answers.

Another plan, where there are no questions and
answers, is to assign individual lines or stanzas to certain
tables or rows. An artistic cumulative effect can be produced by starting with just one row or table, then adding
another on the second stanza, and adding another on each
of the subsequent stanzas or parts. The volume increases
naturally, and a dramatic crescendo results. Solo parts
can be given to various children in turn, with consideration
of need for attention, skill in reading, or type of voice.

The pupils in general, or a small, silent audience-
group can make suggestions after the verses have been read.
"How can we do it another way?" is the question. A surprising number of variations can be obtained by changes in
organization, volume, pitch, speed, emphasis, and legato
or staccato style.

The copies, whether on a chart or mimeographed,
should be preserved and gradually accumulated. As in
music class, the choral reading session can begin with
reading of an old favorite, followed by learning to read a
new selection effectively.

The benefits are many. Children gain in reading
skills, in appreciation of literature, and in ability to work
together. They learn to read creatively, trying several
methods of rendition to achieve the author's and their own
purposes. Pronunciation and enunciation improve. Shy or
aggressive children forget their own problems and are taken
up in the group effort. Several choral reading periods a
week should be part of the urban program.

Dramatics

As early as 1962, when educators and psychologists
were just becoming aware of the problem of the urban child,
Riessman[12] called attention to the value of dramatics.
Teachers who have followed his suggestion agree that dramatics is an especially successful teaching and learning aid
for the disadvantaged.

A natural form of dramatics is the spontaneous role-
playing of kindergarten children. The teacher provides a few
properties, such as a pair of men's shoes, a necktie, a
woman's purse, a toy sink and stove, and a cradle with a
baby doll in it. Given access to this housekeeping corner,

the kindergarten children will assume family roles. "You be
the father; I'll be the mother; and this is our baby." Or
Daddy may go off to work while mother goes marketing, returns, and cooks dinner. There is, of course, no reading
in this role-playing, but it is natural for all children and
serves as a forerunner of dramatized readings in later grades.

The next step is creating a play from material in the
basal reader, or from a story the teacher has read to the
class. The Billy Goats Gruff is an excellent one to start on
since it has one locale, a clearly structured plot, and characters (the goats and the troll) which help the children to
forget self-consciousness.

The teacher must preplan these plays at first--number
of scenes, number of characters, a few costume bits for
ready identification of the characters (a paper crown for a
king; a red coat or jacket for Little Red Riding Hood), and
arrangement of furniture to fit the story. If the teacher's
desk is center front, it should be pushed over to one side
unless it performs some function in the play.

The class will read or hear the story with the teacher,
plan for scenes, characters, properties, and costume pieces,
with the teacher's preplanning available if the children are
unable to make necessary suggestions.

There will be much motivated reading here--skimming
and rereading to clarify certain parts as well as going to
other sources to check on details. Children gradually learn
to outline the scenes, to set the "stage," and to improvise
dialogue. The teacher's planning serves only as a guide in
helping the children to work out their own solutions. Creative drama is useful in all grades in elementary and secondary
school, and even in college classes.

Classic books in the field of creative dramatics are
Children's Literature for Dramatization: An Anthology[13] and
Creative Dramatics: An Art for Children,[14] both written by
Geraldine Brain Siks. Based on twenty years of work with
children, the first book contains adaptations of eighty poems
and fifty stories classified as Poetry Inviting Action, Poetry
Inviting Characterization, Poetry Motivating Conflicts, Stories
for Young Children, and Stories for Older Children. The
second book, Creative Dramatics, is addressed to the teacher
and provides rationale, preparation, and procedures for
leading children to creative performances.

Plays as Teaching Tools in the Elementary School, by
Diane Bordan,[15] is another book to help the teacher. She
recounts, step by step, her own experiences in creating plays
with children in various grades and of different reading levels.
Her suggestions are particularly valuable for the teacher
whose pupils are unable to read their social studies textbooks.
Many of the plays also serve guidance functions. This is
serendipity--guidance help for children with problems, and
establishment of background for understanding social studies,
both at the same time that reading skills are improved through
creative dramatics.

Recently, publishers have begun to include plays in
their reading textbooks. The Oral Reading and Linguistics[16]
series, published by Benefic Press, is a good example. Some
of the stories are told with the traditional "he said, she said"
form of dialogue, whereas others list the character speaking
in the left margin and include only words actually spoken in
the text. This format is especially useful in urban schools,
so that the pupils can take an active part in reading without
having to struggle with descriptions and other obstacles to
finding the dialogue.

Another good source for dramatics by older children
is the On the Telephone[17] series published by Teachers College Bureau of Publications. The situations are ones with
which the reader can identify, and word-calling is reduced
because of the telephone setup and the interest of the material.
Such dramatic readers are recommended for reluctant or retarded urban readers who gain in comprehension by this
means. The pleasure they take in reading is evident, and
since there is no audience, except other pupils in the same
class, there is no tension in the situation.

The magazine, Plays, issued ten times a year, contains plays for younger and for older children which are free
of royalties for subscribers. Non-subscribers must write to
the editorial office for permission to use these plays. A
copy in the school library may be a fruitful source of material for assembly programs. There are also playlets occasionally included in The Instructor and Teacher (formerly The
Grade Teacher).

The final type of dramatics is formal theatre. This
consists of printed lines which the characters must memorize.
Artistically-gifted children prepare the scenery; P.T.A. members and other mothers sew the costumes. The finished

production is given at a regular assembly in the auditorium, or for the parents as one of the events of the year. The amount of tension generated for teacher and pupils is the principal objection to formal dramatics. The time taken from other subject areas is another drawback. Perhaps a drama club for children interested in this type of activity would offer a solution.

Reading Aloud by the Teacher

When we consider the few occasions on which adults are called upon to read aloud, we may well wonder if oral reading in the curriculum is necessary at all. As preparation for adult life, it is probably not. As a learning activity to improve reading skills, appreciation of literature, and general attitudes toward school, it decidedly is. Both choral reading and dramatics make important contributions. A third activity which deserves at least fifteen minutes a day is reading aloud by the teacher.

For the teacher first trying reading aloud or seeking to improve his skills in the area, Storyteller, by Ramon R. Ross,[18] is recommended. This book offers practical suggestions for reading effectively to a class, or working with flannel boards or puppets as an adjunct to the reading, and includes annotated selections from many sources.

The book the teacher decides to read from may be on a higher level than the present reading achievement of the class. This provides access to enjoyable stories, poems, or other literature which the pupils cannot read for themselves. It also extends their horizons through vicarious experience, their vocabulary by meeting new words in a meaningful setting, and their comprehension by listening in a relaxed setting to the teacher's good reading, rather than losing the thought while trying to puzzle out separate words alone.

On the other hand, the selection chosen may be at, or even a little below, the class reading level, in order to interest reluctant and retarded readers in books they can later read comfortably for themselves.

Evidence that oral reading by the teacher is helpful to the pupils may be found in a study by Cohen.[19] Using children in a deprived neighborhood, she arranged for twenty experimental classes to hear a story read aloud each day for fifty days. The control group had its regular basal reader lessons, with the teacher occasionally reading a story aloud for a treat.

The books chosen for the experimental group had to meet the following criteria:

1. Events, concepts, and relationships had to be within the scope of a young child's conceptual grasp.

2. The stories had to allow for emotional identification with the characters.

3. The stories should be written in natural language which would convey precise ideas and colorful images. There were no stipulations regarding vocabulary, length of words, and types of sentences.

A panel of judges selected the books and indicated by 1, 2, or 3 the level of difficulty. The teachers were asked to read the books to the class in the order of their difficulty. A manual of optional follow-up activities was provided.

The children in the experimental and the control groups were tested in October and again in June on all three parts of the Metropolitan Achievement Test, Upper Primary, and on a Free Association Vocabulary Test.

The gains made during the year showed that the experimental classes had a greater increase in vocabulary than the control group (significance .005). On the Word Knowledge section of the Metropolitan Test, the difference, in favor of the experimental classes, was significant at the .005 level after completion of the investigation. In Reading Knowledge on the Metropolitan Test, the difference in favor of the experimental group's gains was significant at the .01 level. The six lowest ability classes also made significant gains as compared with the control group. This research study lends itself to ready replication and should be carried out in other grades to test its results with older pupils.

Conclusion

Whatever the loss to other subject areas, fifteen

minutes a day should be devoted to choral reading and another
fifteen minutes to hearing the teacher read aloud. Creative
dramatics should be used frequently in connection with reading and with social studies. In addition, a sizable amount
of time should be allotted to individualized or supplementary
reading so that every child has a means of increasing his
vocabulary and rate of reading.

Choral reading should be included for its interest,
flexibility, and bettering of pupils' reading and speaking
skills. Dramatics should be used because it contributes to
self-expression, creativity, comprehension, and other reading skills. Reading by the teacher is necessary for the
pupils to associate pleasure with books, to introduce them
to a wide variety of literature, and to increase vocabulary
and develop concepts.

Notes

1. James Hoetker, Dramatics and the Teaching of Literature.
   Champaign, Illinois: National Council of Teachers of
   English, 1969, p. 6.

2. Emmett Albert Betts, Foundations of Reading Instruction.
   New York: American Book Co., 1950, p. 514.

3. John V. Gilmore, Gilmore Oral Reading Test. Yonkers-
   on-Hudson, New York: World Book Co., 1951.

4. William S. Gray, The Gray Oral Reading Tests. Indian-
   apolis: The Bobbs-Merrill Co., 1959.

5. Edward William Dolch, Methods in Reading. Champaign,
   Illinois: Garrard Press, 1955, pp. 44-58.

6. Betts, op. cit., pp. 515ff.

7. Albert J. Harris, How to Increase Reading Ability. New
   York: Longmans, Green and Co., 1956, p. 186.

8. Harris, op. cit., pp. 423-432.

9. Grace Gorgas Cukras, "A Critical Study of the Prosodic
   Elements of Intensity and Pauses as Related to Reading Comprehension at the Intermediate Grade Level."
   Unpublished Doctoral dissertation, Fordham University,
   1973.

10. Louise B. Scott and Jesse J. Thompson, Rhymes for
    Fingers and Flannelboards. New York: McGraw
    Hill and Co., 1960.

11. May Hill Arbuthnot and Shelton L. Root, Jr., Time for
    Poetry. Glenview, Illinois: Scott, Foresman and
    Co., 1968.

12. Frank Riessman, The Culturally Deprived Child. New
    York: Harper and Brothers, 1962.

13. Geraldine Brain Siks, Children's Literature for Drama-
    tization. New York: Harper and Row, 1964.

14. _____, Creative Dramatics: An Art for Children.
    New York: Harper and Brothers, 1958.

15. Diane Bordan, Plays as Teaching Tools in the Elemen-
    tary School. West Nyack, New York: Parker
    Publishing Co., 1970.

16. Mildred A. Dawson and Georgiana Newman, Oral Reading
    and Linguistics. Westchester, Illinois: Benefic
    Press, 1969.

17. Richard H. Turner, When People Talk...On the Tele-
    phone. New York: Teachers College, Columbia
    University, 1964.

18. Ramon R. Ross, Storyteller. Columbus, Ohio: Charles
    E. Merrill Publishing Co., 1972.

19. Dorothy Cohen, "The Effect of Literature on Vocabulary
    and Reading Achievement," Elementary English, 45
    (February, 1968), 209-213, 217.

4. TAXONOMY OF PROBLEMS OF THE ECONOMICALLY DISADVANTAGED YOUNG CHILD

Anne H. Adams and R. Baird Shuman

During the last decade, one of the first tasks under-taken in establishing programs for economically disadvantaged children was to identify the specific problems of children who come from disadvantaged homes to pre-primary or graded schools. Educators, sociologists, and psychologists became the primary consultants who offered advice, recommendations, suggestions, and conclusions concerning the disadvantaged child in numerous planning and developmental sessions with administrators and teachers of disadvantaged children. Some of these authorities had never lived as economically disadvantaged children or adults, and their studies had been primarily vicarious observations and research of overt conditions and behavioral patterns. Ironically, the authorities probably knew from first hand experience less about conditions of poverty than their audiences.

During 1968, a research study was undertaken to determine what problems were identified by teachers or teacher's aides working with underprivileged children. The adult participants in the study had at one time lived in economically disadvantaged homes, and the participants were working only with children from disadvantaged homes.

The 62 participants met in three different groups on three different occasions, and this paper is a report of the results of those meetings. The authors have used the cate-gorical statements of the participants, and presented their expressions of details with reference to each problem cate-gory. The following problems were identified as primary

Anne H. Adams and R. Baird Shuman, "Taxonomy of Problems of the Economically Disadvantaged Young Child," Malaysian Journal of Education (June 1972), pp. 68-74. Reprinted by permission of the authors and publisher.

concerns of economically disadvantaged children in their
order of inclusion in the discussions:

GROUP ONE (23 participants)

    1. Adjusting to a New Baby: When a new baby
arrived, there were less food and space in the home.
Diminished attention was given to the older children, who,
in many instances, received little personal attention prior
to the arrival of the new baby.

    2. Eating: This problem was identified both in the
area of children who did not have a variety of foods to eat,
and therefore were placed on a restricted diet, and in the
area where children did not learn how to manipulate foods
because eating utensils were not provided in the home. In
many homes, children eat with their fingers from a common
plate.

    3. Joining in the Group: This problem was particu-
larly acute for those children who came from large families
where close identification was usually with only the immediate children in the family. When a child who knew only the
children in his family entered school, he simply did not
know how to adjust to a different group of children. This
was particularly noticeable with children from sparsely popu-
lated rural areas, and with the only child in a home who had
played by himself most of the time prior to entering school.

    4. Thumbsucking: No attempt was made to identify
the reason for this characteristic of some children from disadvantaged homes; however, many children in the classroom
were thumbsuckers.

    5. Sharing: This problem was observed primarily in
one of two ways: (1) the child who refused to share and
wanted everything he could grasp for himself; and (2) the child
who took little interest in any activity and was an isolate.

    6. Selfishness: Some children wanted to hoard or
possess material items. This problem, although related to
the sharing problem, was different in that the child classified
as selfish took no interest in other children.

    7. Nervousness: Although the symptoms varied
according to the child, a change in the teacher's voice from

soft to loud usually produced some nervous response on the
part of the child. The children jumped and appeared frightened when a loud noise was heard in the room.

8. Recognizing Danger: Because of the restricted
environments of many of the children, danger signals were
unknown to them, and there had been little home education
or conditioning for safety measures.

9. Listening: In addition to short attention spans,
listening was handicapped by the low vocabulary knowledge
of children from many economically disadvantaged homes.

10. Manners: Cultural responses, commonly de-
noted as "good manners," were not a characteristic of
many economically disadvantaged children. Particularly
noticeable were the gross behavior of children at mealtime,
their responses to overtures of adults, and their care of
property.

11. Coördination: The inability of the children to
use crayons, pencils, and to build towers of blocks was
specifically traced to lack of coördination. The basic cause
of the problem was a lack of emphasis in the home on using
manipulative objects.

12. Cleanliness: The problem of lack of cleanliness
was increased by situations in inadequate washing facilities
in the home, few changes of clothing for the children, and
parents who did not help their children develop habits of
cleanliness.

13. Temper: Flare-ups of temper, evidenced by
sudden fighting, biting, clawing, or yelling were the most
common reactions noted by the teachers and teacher's aides.
This problem seemed to be more closely related to lack of
sharing than to any other reason.

14. Dressing: Tying shoes, buttoning buttons, and
zipping zippers were major handicaps to children. Teaching
these actions took a long time.

15. Home: The attitudes and apathy of parents in
the home as well as home conditions from a material standpoint were noted. Alcoholism, friction among family members, wasteful use of money, and the absence of one parent
were the most commonly noted probable causes of school

responses or lack of responses on the parts of some children.

16. Following Directions: Directions stated to children in one to three words were most likely to be followed; however, when the directions involved several actions and many words, the children became confused.

17. Stubbornness: Some children refused to respond to individual requests or to coöperate in group activities. Many children were uncoöperative and were considered "stubborn" in their actions because they did not understand the requests.

18. Bully: The power of an individual displayed in strong and sometimes cruel terms was termed bullying. Several adults agreed the child who was a bully had been taught the techniques in the home.

19. Recognizing Objects: Many children experienced difficulty in recognizing and naming objects. Rarely would the children invent terms for the objects and communication was limited.

20. Death: When a death occurred in the family, the children did not understand; yet, most young children attended funerals.

21. Poverty: To the child from a poverty home, the effects of poverty itself were most brutal when the child saw material items that he did not and could not have.

22. Sleeping: Physical deficiencies and staying awake late hours at night were evidenced by children going to sleep in class. On the other hand, hyperactive children did not want to rest during rest time in class.

23. Lack of Love: Children who received little attention at home were usually either overly possessive of their teacher and rarely left her side, or conversely were antagonistic toward their teacher.

GROUP TWO (18 participants)

1. Home Environment: The home environments of many children included inadequate heating and clothing, absent father, nagging mother, insufficient food, quarrels among

family members, and children left unattended by adults.

2. Negligent Parents: Although the problem of the
parent who neglects his child is in some cases closely identified with the home environment, the problem of negligent
parents was severe to the extent that it was included sepa-
rately. Specific instances of parental neglect included parents
who did not get their children dressed for school or give them
breakfast before leaving for school; parents who could not or
would not help their children with homework; parents who
were too tired or too busy to talk with their children or to
answer their questions; and parents who were rarely at home.

3. Conforming to Behavior of Society: The children
who experienced difficulty with this problem included those
who were told they could not play with children from other
social strata and who were not allowed to play with others
outside their immediate environment; children who were over-
protected by parents and not allowed out of their sight; and
children who were punished for behavior that was not characteristic of a subservient standard.

4. Partiality of Close Relatives: In some homes, one
child was favored and the other children in the home were
not given specific favors. For example, one child cried and
received immediate attention; another child cried, and no one
in the family seemed to care. Another example cited was
the child who would hurt other children in the family and not
be punished, as contrasted with another child's in the family
receiving punishment for the same offense. There were instances of relatives' intervening in school in behalf of a child
and in opposition to the wishes of the teacher.

5. Rejected Child: Children who have physical de-
formities have been known to be rejected--especially if the
deformity is easily visible, like a birthmark on the face.
In some instances one child from the family accompanies the
adults to the town or a neighbor's home while the other children are repeatedly not chosen to leave the home on short
trips. Handicapped children are at times rejected by the
other children in the class, especially during play periods.
Children have been known to be locked out of the house, usually as a result of anger on the part of the parents. In cases
where the parents are busy and the child is an only child, he
feels rejected when his loneliness becomes almost constant.

6. Criticism in the Home: Parents who were critical

of the school and its teachers were cited as the major problem in this area. Children who accidentally break or mar
some object in the home may be criticized without apparent
understanding or reference to the fact that the matter was an
accident. Particularly does this become a problem for the
child when he is actually trying to do something to receive
praise, and instead, receives criticism. Children who cannot
please their parents are often shy and retiring in the classroom.

   7. Cruelty: Specific instances of cruelty to children
included whipping the child and sending him to bed without
dinner as a result of a minor offense. The cruelty was increased when the child was sent to school the following morning and the adult did not give him his breakfast. Child
neglect was cited as an instance of specific cruelty to children. Transference of fear from fear of parents to fear of
all adults had been observed in teacher-child conferences.
Lack of communication between parent and child was another
instance of cruelty to the child.

   8. Mismanagement of Money: Spending money on
whiskey, expensive automobiles, and gadgets when the need
was for food, clothing, and improved shelter was the major
factor associated with the money problem. In some instances
ADC checks were thought to be spent by the parent for the
adult's pleasure instead of providing the child with basic living
necessities. On the other hand, the money may be spent to
buy a machine, such as an automatic washing machine; yet the
child's clothes were dirty. Money spent on luxury foods when
a balanced diet was needed; parents' gambling away of food
stamps; parents' riding in a new automobile when there was
not enough food at home were other instances of mismanagement of money.

   9. Poverty: Have-not children may watch the
have children buy ice cream cones, and the have-not's have
no ice cream cone money. Children in poverty may live in
shacks; yet, they observe the better homes of other children.
Children in poverty may sleep in a bed with three or four
other children, and food is scarce and often monotonous in
its sameness. Children in poverty may have a cold biscuit
and sausage in their lunch sacks and watch the other children
eating a school cafeteria lunch.

   10. Lack of Attention: A child who seems to have no
one to care for him; a child whose parents are intoxicated

most of the time; a child who receives few responses from
adults in the home; a child who is more often sad than
happy was the description given to children whose major
problem is lack of attention.

11. Non-support: Specific instances of non-support
included mothers and children abandoned by fathers and
having no immediate means of support; children abandoned
in the home with no food and no indication of when the parent
would return; children in a home that has the bare essentials
to live and in which the adults have no incentive to improve
the situation; children who are deprived because the father
uses any earned money for gambling.

12. Mental Retardation: Children who are mentally
retarded often did not play with other children because the
other children would not play with them. Some parents simply did not know what to do with or for the child who is mentally retarded. More often than not, mentally retarded children were ignored in the home and rarely were taken outside
the home.

13. Boredom: A child whose problem was simply
being bored may have few toys and may be alone at home
with nothing to do. He may be told to watch a television
program that is not interesting to him or is above his level
of comprehension. In general, such a child was left to his
own devices; and, when there were few areas to broaden his
environment, the child became bored.

14. Domination of Adults: Adults who make children
conform by brute force was the first instance cited as an act
of adult domination of a child. In some homes, children wait
until after the adults have finished eating before the children
can eat what is left. Diversions may be based on adult interests rather than on the interests of the child.

15. Untruthful Parents: Parents who continue to
promise children items that they know cannot be delivered
may produce a basic lack of trust and security in the child.
Some parents go to town to buy new clothes for the children
and instead come home intoxicated, and with no new clothes.
Parents may promise to take a child on a trip, and never get
around to taking the child.

16. Desertion of Parents: Children had been given
away by their parents, and the children knew the parents did

not want them. The absence of the father in the home might
be an act of permanent desertion of the family; occasionally
the same reason applied to the absence of the mother.

17. Over-Protective Parents: Parents who will not
send their children to school because the children would be
away from home; parents who would not let their children
play with other children because they were afraid of acci-
dents; a parent who cried when the child left for school because the child would be gone from home for a period of
time; and parents who would not let their children play because they were afraid the child's clothes would get dirty
were instances cited concerning over-protective parents.

18. Fear: Children who were afraid to go anywhere
unless the mother was along; children who would not play
with other children because they were afraid the children
would laugh at their appearance; children who were afraid to
ride on the school bus; and children who were afraid of the
dark exemplified the problem of fear.

GROUP THREE (21 participants)

1. Cleanliness: Some children did not know how to
use the paper towels furnished by the school. In cases where
the homes of the children were unsanitary, bed clothing was
usually dirty; children slept in the same clothes they wore to
school. The children smelled unpleasant and the odor of the
home was also unpleasant.

2. Adjusting to School: The child's first contact with
a person representing the school was the bus driver, in many
instances. Bus drivers commented that in some cases, the
children felt the adult bus driver was the person with whom
they should remain. They hesitated to leave the bus and
walk into a strange building. Many started to cry at this
point. Other school adjustment problems included their not
knowing how to use the bathrooms at school; their playing by
themselves because they were afraid of or did not know how
to play with other children; and their throwing toys because
they did not know how to play with the toys.

3. Manners: Observation of the lack of manners was
observed primarily in the cafeteria where children turned
their faces from the children in the group; children ate too
fast--probably to make sure the food was not taken away; and

posture at the table was haphazard. At times children who
did not speak were found to have speech impediments and
laughter from other children frequently occurred when the
child spoke. As a result, these children often did not respond orally, and the lack of response was sometimes con-
strued to mean the child was rude.

4. Aversion to Vegetables: The three vegetables
most often mentioned by the cafeteria workers that were not
chosen by the children to eat were carrots, English peas,
and corn. Of all foods served, vegetables more often than
any other food were not eaten. Milk, surprisingly, was not
drunk by a number of children. The children either did not
like the taste of whole milk served at school because they
were accustomed to the taste of dried milk mixed at home,
had not had milk at home and were unaccustomed to its taste,
or did not know how to manage the milk in unaccustomed
containers.

5. Talking: The children did not know how to "share"
talking, and this was evidenced either by their talking all at
one time or by the raising of voice levels of some children so
they would be heard over the voices of the other children.
Conversely, the child who did not talk was considered to have
problems. Again, speech impediments, primarily stuttering,
were thought to be the reason for the child's refusal to talk.
As one adult stated, "Some children don't talk because they
think their words won't come out right."

6. Hunger: Some children ran to the table to eat
and began to "wolf" their food. Some children who were crying, when questioned, would state their stomachs hurt because
they were hungry. At times children had hunger headaches,
yet were sitting before plates filled with food, but refusing to
eat the food because they did not like the taste of the food.

7. Improper Clothing: Children who wore ragged,
torn, or ill-fitting clothes frequently elected to play together.
Rarely did a child with old clothes play with a child who was
well-dressed. Children wearing ill-fitting clothes were often
snubbed by the children whose clothes were well chosen.
Some parents sent their children to school in cold weather
without regard to dressing them in warm clothing, and at
times even shoes were absent on cold days.

8. Lack of Attention: Baby sitters may not be provided in the homes when the parents leave at night--unless

the baby sitter is an older brother or sister or an adult relative who lives in the home.   In some instances everyone in
the home has something to do except the young child, and this
child is left to his own devices.   In some cases misbehavior
is deliberately caused by the child who wants to attract attention to himself.

9. Stubbornness: Children classified as stubborn
were those who did not want to go to bed when told to do so;
refused to obey the parent or teacher; did not want to stop
playing--or fighting--with other children; and did not want to
go to the chalkboard in the classroom to participate in classroom activities.

10. Habits: Some children developed a habit of fighting as an automatic reaction to their displeasure.   Other
habits of a problem nature included waiting to go to the bath-
room until it was too late (a frequent happening), eating from
the tray with their hands, and thumb sucking.

11. Home Bound: Children who had rarely left home
prior to going to school had been known to cry because they
could not play with other children or were unhappy because
they could not visit other children who were allowed to visit
their homes.   In some cases, the children were allowed to
ride in the car to a store, but were not allowed to enter the
store and were told to wait in the car.   These children saw
the exteriors, but rarely the interiors of buildings.

12. Not Sharing: Instances of inability to share concerned a toy, particularly a ball, a truck, or a doll.   Some
children attempted to gather all of the toys and defy other
children to try to play with them.   When a rope was in the
classroom, the children might pull on the rope--not as enter-
tainment--but to have possession of the rope.

13. Fear: The greatest fear that could be observed
in the classroom from an overt standpoint was fear of the
doctor or nurse who came to the school to give shots.   Some
children were afraid of the water in the commode.   The sight
of a bottle of medicine produced crying from many children.

14. Quarreling: A book has prompted many quarrels
among the children.   If one child was looking at the book and
another child became interested in it, more often than not a
quarrel resulted.   Quarrels between the parent and the child
prior to the child's leaving home usually are concerned with

the parent's whipping the child at home to make the child go
to school. Quarrels between parents in the early morning
hours or between parents and other children in the home are
frequently noted by the children.

        15. Sleeping: Although one recommendation for pre-
primary classroom is to have a rest time, many children do
not lie down on the mats provided for this purpose. Some
will sit on the mats, and some children request pillows.
Many children do not have pajamas at home.

        16. Partiality of Parents: The teen-agers or older
children may receive a new article or articles of clothing
while the younger children do not receive new clothes. The
younger children do not understand this. In some instances,
a child in the home will cry and receive immediate attention
from the parent--and another child in the same home cries
and receives no attention from the parent. Some children,
usually the older ones, are allowed to accompany the parent
to a store where the child receives candy or an inexpensive
toy. Seldom are candy and toys bought for the children who
remain at home.

        17. Home Life: Children who ask questions of par-
ents who cannot, do not, or will not answer the questions may
themselves not ask questions at school and rarely engage in
conversation with the teacher. Children who do not have toys
of their own at home may evidence an inability to share at
school or a lack of knowledge about how to play with the toys
provided at school.

SUMMARY AND RECOMMENDATIONS

        Similarities and differences have been noted with
reference to the problems identified by three different groups
of participants. In some instances, a major problem identified by one group was a minor example of a major problem of
another group.

        The problems of the economically disadvantaged child
are apparently related to environmental, financial, or physical and mental development. The teachers felt handicapped
in helping the child with problems contained within or stem-
ming from the home. The basic question of how far the
school can attempt to help children solve their problems remains unsolved. For example, when alcoholism is a problem

in the home, what can the school do to help a young child who is suffering from the effects of this problem in his home?

The major need stated by the teachers and aides with reference to helping the children is for the development of classroom instructional materials to help them help the children. They did not have access to instructional materials designed to cope with elimination of social problems. In fact, the solution of classroom disturbances and other problems of children have been left to the voice and creative thinking of the teachers. The need is for the pre-primary or graded curriculum to include educationally sound materials and methodologies to help in the elimination of the learning and self-concept problems that are probable causes of future impediments to success for many children.

5. NEW MATHEMATICS AND OLD TEACHERS IN THE ELEMENTARY SCHOOL

W. M. Perel and Philip D. Vairo

A great deal of attention has been given during the past few years to a phenomenon known simply, if incorrectly, as the "new math." But very little attention has been given to those teachers who are always called upon to implement any changes in school curriculum.

It has been pointed out many times that the so called "new math" is not really very new and even that there is no such word as "math," but the expression "new math" seems to be with us and will probably stay with us. It should be added that there is no one simple set of curricular experiences in mathematics which is identified by this phrase. But all of these curricular experiences are new to a great many of the teachers expected to teach them.

One might assume that those persons now being trained to be elementary school teachers are properly prepared. However, an examination of the training being given at many universities demonstrates that such an idea is utopian. The Committee on the Undergraduate Program (CUPM) of the Mathematical Association of America has made a study of the mathematical needs of prospective elementary school teachers and has published its recommendations. The recommendations call for three semester courses in mathematics, especially designed for the prospective elementary school teacher containing, in addition to the standard topics of set theory and arithmetic, some instruction in geometry. Yet in only a handful of colleges and universities do we find more than one semester course in mathematics, especially for

W. M. Perel and Philip D. Vairo, "New Mathematics and Old Teachers in the Elementary School," Educational Forum (March 1967), pp. 345-348. Reprinted by permission of the authors and publisher.

elementary teachers. Indeed, in some universities even this
one special course is lacking or has nothing to do with the
CUPM recommendations.

But the mathematical preparation of those elementary
school teachers already in service gives even greater concern, because there are more of them, their training is even
more meager, and such as it is, even more remote. During
the academic year 1965-1966, one of the authors, W. M.
Perel, directed an In-Service Institute in mathematics for
elementary school teachers, supported by the National Science
Foundation on the campus of the University of North Carolina
at Charlotte. The sixty-seven applicants had experience
ranging from one year to over fifteen years, with an approxi-
mate average of eight years. Most of these teachers will
continue to teach in elementary schools for at least the next
twenty years. What can be said about their preparation for
teaching mathematics?

Table I below shows the mathematical training these
teachers have received. Observe that twenty-three teachers
had no college work in mathematics whatever, not even a
mathematics methods course. In conversation with these
teachers the authors learned that many of them took only
the required minimum mathematics in high school, which certainly included no geometry or intermediate algebra. With

Table I.* Distribution of Mathematics Courses
of Applicants Who Applied to the
National Science Foundation Institute at the
University of North Carolina at Charlotte

Courses	Number	Percent
Mathematics Education or Teaching of Arithmetic	19	28. 4
Commercial Mathematics	3	4. 5
Algebra	9	13. 4
Algebra--Trigonometry	12	17. 9
Algebra--Trigonometry--Calculus	1	1. 5
No courses in any of the above	23	34. 3
Total	67	100. 0

*Data obtained from NSF Institute applications.

these teachers, the problem is not a lack of training in new
mathematics, but a lack of training in mathematics, new or
old.   Of the remaining teachers most had not had a course
in what could be called modern mathematics.

Of the teachers who applied for admission to this
Institute, fifteen, or twenty-two per cent, held a master's degree and might, therefore, be expected to occupy a position
of leadership in the elementary school. However, these teachers did not have better preparation in mathematics than did
the others.   Fourteen out of the fifteen teachers holding the
master's degree received it in graduate education and had no
graduate course work in mathematics.   The other degree was
in theology.

Only two of the sixty-seven teachers stated that they
read the Arithmetic Teacher or any other journal, magazine,
or book which would assist them in carrying out their teaching assignments in mathematics.   The National Science Foundation with its support of In-Service and Summer Institutes
for elementary school teachers has attempted the task of retraining.   But during 1965-1966 the National Science Foundation
was only able to support forty In-Service Institutes for elementary school teachers in mathematics in the whole country.   The
one held at the University of North Carolina at Charlotte was
the only one in the Carolinas.   It has been estimated that if
the National Science Foundation programs for elementary
school teachers remain at their present size, only a minority
of the elementary school teachers now in service would be able
to have an Institute experience at any time during the next
fifty years.

Colleges and universities can and in some cases have
rendered assistance in the retraining of elementary school
teachers without outside support.   However, many institutions
have not offered suitable courses in the past and have not
encouraged elementary school teachers in sufficient numbers
to avail themselves of opportunities that do exist.

It is true that many school districts operate "workshops" for elementary school teachers in mathematics, as
well as in other disciplines.   But workshops, in the opinion
of both authors, are generally unsatisfactory, in spite of the
fact that teachers generally like them.   Usually their duration
is short, they require little preparation and sometimes little
thought.   Often too much attention is devoted to gadgets, toys,
and other such devices.   Important as visual aids are, an

examination of them does not take the place of training in mathematics, nor is it a remedy for a lack of such training. It would seem that elementary school teachers must learn some mathematics, if they are to teach it. Retraining is the term usually used, but it must be recognized that in many cases the training will be the first mathematical experience of the teacher. The authors have no easy solution to so massive a problem as the mathematical training of thousands upon thousands of elementary school teachers now in service. They are convinced that there is no alternative to teachers learning some mathematics.

In a typical elementary school, there are no subject-matter specialists and hence there is likely to be no person, teacher or principal, to offer any form of leadership to a teacher trying to teach what he, himself, may not fully understand. It is true that most of the texts come with either teachers' editions or teachers' manuals, prepared either by the authors of the text themselves or by others. However, most teachers do not find the explanations in their manuals adequate. Certainly a teacher's manual does not and cannot provide an understanding which would be gained by three semesters of study on a university or college campus. Nor is it reasonable to expect them to do so.

As long as the mathematical curriculum was traditional, the teacher had the advantage of knowing where it was intended to lead. Most teachers, even at the lower grade levels, remember the mathematics which they studied in the fifth and sixth grades and even in junior high school, even if they do not understand it. But today, the teacher struggling to teach "new" second grade mathematics has only the vaguest notion of what it is for and to what it will lead in the higher grades. For this reason, as well as for others, many teachers feel that the "new" mathematics is inferior to the old, to which they would gladly return.

The new mathematics has driven teachers to institutes, workshops, and college courses in a state of abject terror at having to teach it. One could wish that they came with a desire and an interest in learning mathematics, but their coming at all is indeed a fringe benefit of the changes in the mathematics curriculum.

Some teachers are aware of the controversy surrounding some of the topics of the so-called "new math" and are filled with glee when they find an article, written by someone

highly placed in mathematics, which is critical of much of
what is now being done. But the trend has been established.
The pendulum may swing back as well as forward, but not
all the way back. Each year more schools make the change,
and more teachers face the problem of change. Hopefully,
teachers will recognize that the reason teaching is a profession rather than a trade, is that in order to continue its
practice, they must continue to learn.

6. TO TAKE A STAR:
TEACHING LITERATURE IN URBAN ELEMENTARY
AND SECONDARY SCHOOLS

Thomas R. Preston

Teaching literature is teaching literature, whether
the students come from rural or urban environments. In
one sense, this assertion is quite true, for a literature
teacher, no matter the environment of the students, is trying to help all students discover how, in what ways, and why
an author uses language to order reality--physical, spiritual,
and psychological. In another sense, the assertion is mis-
leading, especially in the case of elementary and secondary
school children.

Reality, however universal its many forms and structures, also includes the specific data of some cultural milieu.
Literature deals with universals of reality, but it does so
usually by referring to the specific data. A reader encounters,
first, particular images, characters, actions, and plots of
the stories, poems, and plays he is reading, and these par-
ticulars generally reflect the specific data of a cultural milieu.
One of the major skills needed to read and enjoy literature
is that of recognizing how the specifics used in a literary work
develop universal meanings. An elementary or secondary
school child living in an urban environment may never arrive
at the universal meanings in a literary work, if the literature
he grows up on is so rurally oriented that it does not reflect
the reality he knows in his everyday life. I am not saying
that the urban child should not read literature that draws on
the rural environment, but rather that when he does read it
he should be able to relate the rural specifics to his own
urban specifics and discover how both involve universal actions, characters, plots, and themes. To achieve this goal,
the urban child needs to read good literature that reflects
urban environments and to compare it with good literature

Unpublished paper, included by permission of the author.

reflecting rural environments. And both kinds of literature
should be read in the context of great world literature--East,
West, Third world.   This may sound like an impossible goal,
but it is not so impossible as it seems.

Let me make my underlying assumptions explicit.
First, I am assuming that all children--rural or urban--
should be concerned with literature in school, not "readers,"
whether that literature is traditional oral and written literature read aloud to the child or rewritten for the child's vocabulary or whether it is some of the excellent literature
written especially for children.   William Anderson and Patrick
Goff in A New Look at Children's Literature (Belmont, California: Wadsworth Publishing Co., 1972) note that by the
time a child "has reached his fifth year ... he has already
mastered the essential fundamentals of the symbol system
we call his native language.   The child comes to school ...
with relatively sophisticated syntactical, lexical, and phonetic
abilities.   He understands and uses all parts of language with
a high degree of accuracy" (p. 218).   Moreover, older children in the first grade, according to recent studies, "have
listening vocabularies of twenty thousand words" (pp. 4-5).
Piaget's research demonstrates that between 2 and 7 years
the child shows "the gradual development of symbolic representation or an ability to organize symbols" (p. 222); between 7 and 11 the child develops "a stable picture of 'how
things are' by which he approaches new experiences in meaningful terms" (p. 223); and between 11 and 15 the "child is
... able to think in abstract, logical terms, to speculate on
'what if' questions, and has a highly developed sense of
logic" (p. 223).

        The implication of these statistics is that literature
should replace the "graded" or sequential readers in the
schools, and I am delighted to say this seems to be happen-
ing--gradually--around the country.   At least, in Laramie,
Wyoming my seventh grade daughter is reading a splendid
novel by Robert Lipsyte entitled The Contender, and not
some "advanced" version of Dick, Jane, and Puff.   My
sixth grade daughter, in a different school, is developing her
reading skills on the Houghton Mifflin literature series under
the general editorship of James Moffett, and my fourth grade
son, in still a third school, has been excitedly responding to
his teacher's retelling of Beowulf.

        James Moffett writes, "During the K-6 years attempts
to 'structure' the reading of literature by anything more than

general growth seem pointless. The main thing is to give children a rich mixture of whatever literature they are able and eager to read, without schematizing it or thematizing it" (A Student-Centered Language Arts Curriculum, Boston: Houghton Mifflin, 1968, p. 25). One of the few exceptions I would make to Moffet's thesis is the conscious introduction of literature dealing with urban themes into the literature curriculum of urban schools. I urge this because children's literature, especially that written particularly for children, has had, I think, a tendency to be rurally oriented, perhaps influenced by our recent American past. If children in a growing urban society are not to be "turned off" by literature because it seems at first glance to be "irrelevant," I think it is necessary to vary their reading diet with literature that draws on the specifics of urban life.

A second assumption I make is that reading and enjoying literature demands that all children respond actively either by re-creation in some other medium or by creating a new literary work in written form. Re-creating in other media may involve, for example, dramatizing in class a story or poem or acting out a play. Rewriting, for example, may involve "modernizing" a story, poem, or play--an excellent way for children to discover that universal meanings exist in literature and that patterns of action, plot, character, and theme have universal applications transcending time, place, and cultural milieu. Jeanette H. Whatley describes some delightful literary classroom activities in "Creativity in the Humanities Class" (Today's Education, Vol. 60, No. 9, Dec. 1971, pp. 10-12, 58-59). From the language arts perspective, the creating of a response in written form is especially important. James Moffett expresses this point most forcefully: "Rendering experience into words is the real business of school, not linguistic analysis, or literary analysis, or rhetorical analysis, which are proper subjects only for college" (p. 11).

My final assumption is that despite the various sophisticated approaches to reading literature, the great tradition that understands literature first as an imitation of life (or of reality or of the actions of men) best serves as the starting place for children. This understanding of literature, vexed as it has been throughout history, points at least to the idea that literature orders life by imitating the various structures or relationships that human beings discover, create, and work with as they move from birth to death. The adult may be able to distinguish the particular form a structure takes in a given time, place, and cultural milieu from the universal implications of the structure itself. The child does not necessarily make this distinction and may instead see the specific structures of his life as the only ones. School, for example, may be as limited as Public School 21 on the corner of Elm and Main. And this factor should be exploited. Anderson and Goff write that to the child one of the most important aspects of literature "is the reflection of one's own life that literature provides--the insights into identity and existence which emerge from literary portrayal" (p. 224). The implication of this observation, I think, is that for urban children we begin with literature whose particular structures are drawn from the urban environment.

To carry out the goals I have outlined requires that the teacher actively collect a good selection of poetry, fiction, and drama that uses urban and rural environments (a starting place would be the superb annotated bibliography in Anderson and Goff). It also requires that the teacher acquaint the children with a great variety of world stories, so that they can see and compare universal patterns of action, character, and themes. This may mean reading to the class at appropriate intervals from various children's retellings of the Iliad and Odyssey, the Bible, and the Arthurian romances, and from such books as Hero Tales from Many Lands (edited by Alice Hazeltine) or Maria Leach's The Rainbow Book of American Folktales and Legends. By introducing the ancient legends, tales, folktales, and Bible stories in juxtaposition with a modern children's story, the urban child can begin to see how the specifics of time, place, and cultural milieu are used by authors to express universal concerns of men--and of himself in his own urban environment. The urban child can learn to see "the relationship of actual life to its representation in literature.... The child's exclamation, 'That's me!' confirms the affective impact, which depends, of course, on the child's own experiences" (Anderson and Goff, pp. 225-226).

As the great world myths become an informing context for the urban child who is learning to read and enjoy literature, a large part of the actual reading pattern should involve the counterpointing of urban and rural specifics in literature. In poetry, for example, the child can learn to see how the poet's language fuses and separates the specifics of the urban and rural environments to project universal meanings about nature and man. A splendid collection of poetry selected by Nancy Larrick (with the advice of inner-city and small-city children) entitled On City Streets (New York: Bantam Books,

1969), allows this procedure to be easily followed. Using almost any poem in the collection, a teacher can help the child relate urban and rural specifics to each other and to universal meanings. Tom Prideux's lovely poem "Broadway: Twilight" (p. 19), for example, is but eight lines long, and yet it sets up the universal conflict of man and nature in urban rather than rural terms. The first six lines are simply assertions of urban noise and color as they can be perceived at twilight. The "roaring, " "clanking, " and "screaming" of sirens intermixed with the "pink" and "yellow" of the neon signs on Broadway exist at twilight "in confusion" and "in profusion. " But "Above the deepening blue /The stars blink calmly through. " Nature--its color and lights--is calm against the city and man's creation of color and light--noisy and confused. Yet both exist simultaneously, and in the city we are able to experience and enjoy both phenomena, recognizing that nature, which is often thought to be perceived only in the country, can also be reached in the city. The noise of Prideux's Broadway contrasts with the unusual lack of noise offered by the city on Sunday in Phyllis McGinley's "Q is for the Quietness" (p. 31). Silence is personified as a girl who "walks the city /In her pretty velvet shoes. " But breaking the silence with supernatural insistence are "The bells of Sunday morning" that "Ring their questions on the air, " suggesting that in the city we also hear the call to divine things.

The union of man and nature comes into a new focus in Joseph March's "City Autumn" (p. 34). The "frost" of autumn in the city, over whose "grey" streets blow "dust and papers" and "brown leaves" with "curled-up edges, " finds its counterpart in the "frost" of life displayed by an old man tottering past "with a cane /Wondering if he'll see Spring again. " In specifically urban terms, interspersed with nature imagery, March evokes the traditional union of man and nature, wherein the life of both follows the same pattern of "seasonal" development. The same metaphoric fusion occurs in Sanderson Vanderbilt's "December" (p. 79). This poem portrays a little boy shoveling bits of "dirty, soggy snow/ into the sewer-- /With a jagged piece of tin. " Here is a truly urban scene, with inner-city associations about it. But the last lines fuse the action with the universal union of man and nature: "He was helping spring come. " This union of man and nature suggests, in fact, another theme--that of the hero's quest to do some great deed.

Several poems in the anthology are clearly urban

miniatures of the hero's quest. Langston Hughes, for example, treats it in terms of the urban Black's quest for equality in "Mother to Son" (p. 94). The speaker of the poem is an urban Black, a cleaning woman who sees her life in terms of her job--cleaning stairs. "Life for me ain't been no crystal stair," she asserts. Instead, her life of climbing has been on stairs with "tacks," "splinters," "boards torn up," and "places with no carpets on the floor." She tries to pass on to her son her own understanding of life as the climbing of stairs, telling him not to give up and not to "set down on the steps." The universal quest of the hero is here merged with the universal theme of a mother's love, with the mother setting an example for the child to follow: "Don't you fall now-- / For I'se still goin', honey, / I'se still climbin', / And life for me ain't been no crystal stair." In this one short poem a child is confronted with the Black's struggle for equality, a struggle that emerges in the context of an urban slum. Moreover, the struggle also has the overtones of the hero vigorously and relentlessly pursuing a quest in the manner of an Arthurian knight or some other legendary hero--how about Aeneas or Beowulf?

In "Living Among the Toilers" (p. 146), Henri Percikow projects this same quest theme through the eyes of the urban "hard hat" worker who shares the "conveyor belt" and feels the "iron wheel" ride his "bones, / Cruising." But the worker, like Tennyson's Merlin, keeps his eye on the gleam: "My vision clear, / I sing / Of a chromed tomorrow / Held in my calloused palm." With this line the urban worker becomes a knight-errant seeking a future city of "chrome" instead of the rural court of Camelot. But the poem conveys the same heroic quest for fulfillment in life.

The comments on these few poems are not intended to be definitive, but rather to point a direction in the teaching of poetry to the urban child. Perhaps a final set of examples drawn from children's fiction will round out the procedure that I'm suggesting can be used in the urban elementary and secondary schools. These examples involve two fine novels: Ester Weir's The Loner (New York: David McKay, Inc., 1963) and Robert Lipsyte's The Contender (New York: Harper & Row, 1967).

The first of these novels is clearly a rural novel. The main setting is Montana and the story concerns the socializing of a young boy (the loner) into a rural, sheep-herding family. The loner, a motherless and fatherless

crop-picker, learned early in life that "the only way to get
along in the world was to look out for himself" (p. 1). Yet
when a young girl (also a crop-picker) who has befriended
him accidentally dies, we learn that the loner has indeed an
instinctive yearning for others, for "Every inch of his body
ached, ached with weariness and hunger and the terrible
emptiness of losing Raidy" (pp. 15-16). Abandoned in the
wild sheep country of Montana, the loner is found by Boss,
a huge woman who tends the flocks once owned by her son
and seeks to kill the bear who has killed him. After joining
this family consisting of two dogs, the daughter-in-law, Angie,
the hired hand, Tex, and the dominating Boss, the loner begins to learn that life is a quest for fulfillment that involves
a constant battle, but one that can be successfully fought with
the help of others.

The idea of the battle emerges explicitly when Boss,
hesitating about putting some sugar on the loner's mush,
thinks to herself, "Life was a hard business and indulgences
led only to softness, and softness to weakness" (p. 23).
Since the loner has no name, Boss has him select one from
the Bible. He chooses David.

> Her voice was very low. 'You turned to First
> Samuel, chapter sixteen. And put your finger on
> these words, "Send me David thy son, which is
> with the sheep!"
>
> 'That mean my name is David?' She shut the book
> slowly. 'It's a fine name...' He was curious.
> 'Who was he?' 'A shepherd,' Boss said. 'A very
> brave and loyal shepherd. When he was only a boy
> in charge of his father's flock, he risked his life to
> protect his sheep.' (p. 47).

Boss tells the new David the story of the Old Testament David,
reminding him that he now has a name of which to be proud,
but also one that gives him "a lot to live up to" (p. 48). Miss
Weir's allusions to the David story in the Old Testament do
two important things: they establish the novel's theme of the
need for courage and readiness to fight the battle of life and
they associate the battle with the biblical story, thus giving
the contemporary story a universal significance. Later Angie
points out this universal significance to David.

> 'Lots of things in your life can seem pretty over-
> whelming, David. It's not being afraid to try to

conquer that counts ... it's having the faith and
courage that shepherd boy had when he accepted
the challenge. I'm sure you have that courage.'
(p. 53)

Allusions to the Old Testament David continue through
the novel, as David (and the reader) learn an enormous amount
about sheepherding and its difficulties, especially during a
Montana winter. But the socializing of David through the use
of the many specifics about sheepherding is clearly a process
of encouraging him to see that life is a battle that he can
fight with the help of others. At the climax of the story,
David, who has failed in various ways to meet Boss's stand-
ards, attempts to prove his devotion to her and his desire
to fight in the battle of life by killing the bear which has
haunted Boss since her son's death.

'He didn't miss,' Boss said, raising herself on her
elbow. 'I've been lying here thinking about it and
you know what it reminds me of? David in the
Bible, facing up to that giant Goliath with only a
stone in his slingshot. Our David was just like
him--he knew he wouldn't miss.' (pp. 149-150)

David's quest for maturity, fighting the battle of life, is
represented as his meeting the specific challenges of sheepherding, and forms the main action of the novel. Near the
end of the story, as David, now a member of the family, is
preparing to alternate sheepherding with schooling, the narra-
tor describes the locoweed that drives sheep crazy: "City
folk, people who didn't know any better, would look at the
flowers and think how pretty they were. It took a real shepherd to know what they could do to a flock" (p. 151). No
doubt only a "real" shepherd could understand this specific
about the shepherd's life. But the crack about "city folk"
will not pull the wool over the eyes of the urban child who
reads this novel in conjunction with The Contender.

The setting of The Contender is just the opposite from
rural Montana--very urban New York and specifically, Harlem. The hero, a Black youth named Alfred, lives with his
aunt and, like David, he is motherless and fatherless. Alfred
must fight against white prejudice, the slum environment of
Harlem, and the urban Black gang that operates on the principle of stealing because "Whitey been stealing from us for
three hundred years" (p. 5). The physical environment of
Harlem is equally depressing.

The stench of wine and garbage still hung in the
moist June air.   He jammed his hands into the
pockets of his tight blue slacks, watching the cars
cruise past.   Another year, he thought, be eighteen,
able to drive.   Sure.   On grocery-boy pay.   Slave.
(p. 6)

At first glance the two novels would seem to be worlds apart.
But not so.   The story of Alfred follows the same pattern as
the story told about David.   Alfred becomes socialized into
the world, learning that life is a battle that can be fought
with help.

Where the battle of life is depicted in The Loner
through the image of sheepherding, in The Contender it is
depicted through the image of boxing.   Boxing becomes for
Alfred the means he can use to become "someone," to overcome his environment.   When he tells Mr. Donatelli, the
owner of a gym in Harlem, that he wants to be "Somebody
special. A champion" (p. 26), he learns that first he must
become a contender.

Donatelli's thin lips tightened.   'Everybody wants
to be a champion.   That's not enough.   You have
to start by wanting to be a contender, the man
coming up, the man who knows there's a good
chance he'll never get to the top, the man who's
willing to sweat and bleed to get up as high as his
legs and his brains and his heart will take him.'
(p. 27)

A few sentences later Donatelli tells Alfred that "It's the
climbing that makes the man.   Getting to the top is an extra
reward" (p. 27).   Alfred, of course, takes up the "climbing."

Alfred's climb is difficult, and the reader learns an
enormous amount about urban life and about boxing, just as
in The Loner the reader learned about rural Montana and about
sheepherding.   Alfred does not have a biblical counterpart to
give his battle universal meaning; this meaning comes instead
from the Black boxing pantheon.

DONATELLI'S GYM.   Joe Louis had worked out
there once.   He remembered his father talking
about how he had gone over to watch.   Maybe Sugar
Ray Robinson, too.   They weren't no slaves, and
they didn't have to bust into anybody's grocery store.

They made it, they got to be somebody.   (p. 20)

Like David, Alfred receives help--from Henry, Bill Witherspoon, Donatelli--and he becomes not a champion, but a contender, both in boxing and in life. The extension of the boxing image to mean the battle of life is implied throughout the
novel, but it becomes explicit in at least two places. Quoting
Bill Witherspoon, a former contender and now a teacher, to
his cousin, Alfred asserts, "He said if you can concentrate
on learning to box, you can concentrate on learning anything"
(p. 157). Later, Witherspoon describes a trying scene with
one of his students in boxing terms: "I spent the afternoon
trying to explain to him why that knife isn't going to do him
any good. It was like going ten rounds" (p. 167). Alfred's
third and final fight, like David's attack on the bear in The
Loner, proves to all that he has become a contender in the
battle of life. Talking to himself as he takes a merciless
beating in the ring, Alfred resolves that he is "gonna stand
here all day and all night and take what you got and give it
right back, gonna hang in forever, gonna climb, man, gonna
keep climbing, you can't knock me out, nobody ever gonna
knock me out, you wanna stop me you better kill me" (p. 175).

     This brief analysis of The Loner and The Contender
does not pretend to do justice to either novel. As in the earlier
discussion of a few poems from On City Streets, it is intended to point a direction, to indicate a procedure that might
be helpful in teaching literature in the urban elementary and
secondary schools. The procedure tries to utilize the great
literature of the world as a context for reading contemporary
literature. But the reading of contemporary literature is itself approached from an urban perspective that relates the
specifics of urban life to the specifics of rural life, attempting
to show how their study in literature can help the urban child
discover the universal meanings in literature by seeing his
own life and environment reflected there. It can also help
the child discover beneath the differences of urban and rural
specifics a continuity of human concerns and values. Becoming a sheepherder and becoming a contender require similar
strengths and virtues, and these same strengths and virtues
are needed for every hero's quest to become "somebody" in
life.

     I do not wish to claim that the procedure outlined in
this essay is a panacea for teaching literature in urban elementary and secondary schools. It may, however, be useful
in teaching the urban child to discover what value literature

has for himself--to discover that literature may help him fulfill the injunction Langston Hughes gives the "dark boy" in "Stars" (p. 137), the injunction to "Reach up your hand ... and take a star."

7. LET'S MAKE LEARNING FUN IN THE GRADES

Robert J. Krajewski

> I don't like school. All we do is work homework
> problems and listen to the teacher. I never really
> get a chance to get involved. We never have any
> fun in school--it's a total bore!

Too frequently we as teachers effect the above feelings
in our students. We are often at fault for causing students to
drop out of the learning scene at an early age. And why? Do
we unwittingly make learning, even in the early years, a
drudgery or a chore to be contended with? Do we tend to
force learning on our students and in the process frustrate
or bore them? Do we, in fact, tend to take all the fun out
of learning and teaching?

So often we think of fun as being only outside the class-
room--before and after school, or during recess time. Some
of us even feel that fun should stop the minute the child enters school. Now, it is time to work and learn only. How
can these vital aspects be combined in some way? Perhaps
one possibility may be the use of interest centers with our
teaching of skills at any grade level and with any type of
child. If used properly, children love them, are eager to
work with them, learn far more of what we had previously
been trying to force into them, and are frequently heard to
say, "Golly, this is fun!", while at the same time, they are
learning!

An interest center is a valuable component of individualized instruction. It can be a variety of things. It can be a
game children play alone or with others, a crossword puzzle,
or simply a fun gimmick for practicing a specific skill. It
can be part of a learning or activity center. An interest center can be utilized for any age level, in any class and at any

---

Unpublished paper, included by permission of the author.

time of the school year. Its theme may be seasonal or topical, but always functional.   Student participation and involvement are prerequisites, for whatever is used as an interest center, its purpose is to help the child learn by drawing his interests out through doing.

An interest center is an object, normally of multiple parts, which challenges a student to learn and stimulates his interest in a skill within a specific area. It normally asks a question and gives an immediate response to the student's reply. An interest center can be designed utilizing a specific behavioral objective in order to aid the student in the learning process. The interest center should be so designed that it increases the value of the concept on the cognitive and perhaps affective levels.

To be effective, an interest center must elicit participation from the individual student.   It conveys one concept in visual, graphic imagery in such a manner as to draw the individual student to participate in the learning activity.   The center should be arranged so that small groups or individuals can use it without disturbing other students.   The activities should be constructed so that students can participate without the undivided or constant attention of the teacher.

Let us take an example.   A 4th grade self-contained class is working on multiplication facts.   The teacher has constructed an interest center on the bulletin board, entitled "Frog Race."   In the center of the board is a large caricature/picture of a frog.   At the bottom right corner are two pockets.   Each pocket contains multiplication problems.   On the left are two race paths with approximately 10 hurdles. Below each is a small frog pinned to the bulletin board.   The object of the game then is to see which student can win the race, the frog moving up one hurdle as the student gets the problem right.

In the self-contained classroom, several subjects are taught.   The teacher can decide which subject at a given time needs the most emphasis and reinforcement, and then make an interest center for that subject.   The students may use the interest center during the allocated interest center time within the subject area period when it can be most effective.   It is, however, up to the individual teacher to determine what part an interest center will have in the classroom.

What are the guidelines for these teaching aids that

help make the job of teaching easier and the student's response
so positive?

First it is necessary to be aware of the needs of each
child within the classroom in the various subject areas. Any
interest center created by teachers for an individual child or
small group of children needs to have a purpose for the teacher
and for the child. The center must be bright and attractive.
It should be placed where it can be easily reached during
interest center time. Interest centers can be located anywhere in a room--in a learning center area, on the back of
doors, on walls or window shades, or any other space that
can be utilized--for interest centers come in all shapes and
sizes.

Second, after a center is produced it must be introduced to the child or children with whom it is to be used.
This can be done during large group time, small group time,
or individually to those who will use it. Once introduced,
locate it in a certain section of the room where it can be used
during the interest center time. Any interest center should
only remain in operation as long as it is necessary for achieving its purpose. It should then be moved and another center
established. The new interest center may be centered on a
new skill that needs working on, or it may be a different
approach to the same skill. The teacher must always be responsible for evaluating the success or failure of the interest
centers and then responding to correct the ones that are not
serving their purposes. Many interest centers may be used
at any one time depending on the atmosphere of the classroom,
the various levels of students, and their needs. There does,
however, need to be a sense of responsibility of all students
to their teacher and their peers.

Third, interest center time is best operated as part
of the subject taught time. Children should not have unlimited
use, as interest centers need to have indirect supervision or
they may become meaningless to all involved. Interest centers
are not busy work! Their main purpose is teaching while
making it fun for the learner. Creative teacher-made ideas
seem to be most successful, but the occasional commercial
game or activity can be incorporated to fulfill a skill need
and can be successful if introduced and used properly.

Fourth, make interest centers a privilege. If a student
misuses the centers, he loses the privilege for a day or so.
Discipline usually does not have to be a problem if children

are truly interested and know how to use the centers correctly,
and if the centers are geared to their needs and are not left
up beyond the fulfillment of their created purposes.

One important aspect of interest centers is that they
tend to help develop independence and responsibility in children. Not only can they and should they be used at the first
grade level, but they can be incorporated right on through
high school. Centers need to include multi-level activities
and tasks at varying levels of difficulty so as to meet the
needs of the different children in the classroom. Learning
centers are a unique asset to any teacher and classroom; if
they are used properly, learning can be fun. Ask any child
who has been fortunate enough to have spent a year in a
learning center classroom. Learning doesn't have to be cut
and dried; it can be imaginative, it can be a cooperative
venture, it can be just plain fun.

Interest centers in the classroom, to be most bene-
ficial, should be operated in the following manner. Let's
take, for instance, the subject area of reading. One group
of readers may be in a group meeting with their teacher,
another group at their seats doing assigned seatwork, a third
group working with some type of programmed material, and
a fourth group working with interest centers (this also could
include the library table). After a designated amount of time
the groups will switch their various activities.

Is it additional work for the teacher? Yes, indeed--
but in a way, it becomes fun and a challenge to her. It certainly keeps her on her toes when she begins to see the success interest centers bring in children's learning of skills--
heretofore, a grinding process. They begin to make her a
strong believer in fun as a way of learning. The teacher must
always be working on different interest centers to fulfill various skills and levels of needs within her classroom. Each
center must be creative and well thought out. All kinds of
materials can be used; the teacher's imagination is the only
limit. Teacher collaboration is a tremendous idea. Some
can think of ideas, some can draw, some can cut out letters
and some can color in. Sharing of ideas is a good way to
incorporate many different interest centers at various grade
levels.

In summary, interest centers should be designed to:

Involve and interest students in stimulating activities

Nurture initiative and responsibility
Transfer learning
Encourage creative thinking and provide horizontal
    enrichment
Reinforce skills and class presentation
Entertain while educating
Stimulate and support supplementary study and
Test understanding of concepts.

To fulfill the above-stated objectives, they must be:

Changed frequently
Effective in presentation
Neat in appearance and design
Topic-centered
Educational in content and
Relevant to the student's needs.

Teachers in all classrooms, get out your scissors,
your paste, your masking tape, your letters, your magic
markers, your construction paper, poster board, peg-boards,
etc., and, last but not least, your imaginations. Put these
things to work by yourselves or with others, create and manipulate interest centers to fill the needs of the children this
year and every year in your classrooms. Make learning
come alive through fun, eliminate the dull old routines of
yesterday, make next year an opportunity year for all involved.

8. SOCIAL STUDIES FOR DISADVANTAGED YOUTH

Thomas J. Matczynski and Albert G. Leep

The term "disadvantaged youth" has come to the fore-
ground as one of several terms applied to a segment of
society which has been isolated and left behind by certain
social, political, and economic forces and institutions. This
segment of society most affected by these forces consists of
such ethnic minorities as the Puerto Rican, Mexican-American, Negro, American Indian, and the Appalachian white.
Rapid societal changes have affected these subcultures to
such an extent that these people have lost the will as well as
the opportunity to participate in the decision-making processes
of their lives and their country. In recent years the nation
has become increasingly distressed at the prevailing living
conditions and fearful of the possible results of these conditions
for one-third of the nation's population defined as poor. A
multitude of programs have ensued for the alleviation of the
circumstances and behavioral influences associated with poverty. The primary focus of these programs has been directed
toward the younger segment of the above groups. The objective of these programs is to provide the motivational, educational, and economic means by which disadvantaged youths
might wrench themselves free of the fast-hardening cycle of
poverty.

As stated by Isenberg, the "challenge ... is to develop
in the disadvantaged the ability to adjust to a society and a
future for which they are, at present, largely unprepared."[1]
A large portion of this challenge has been projected upon the
elementary schools of the nation.

In spite of the vigorous innovative programs, clamoring

Thomas J. Matczynski and Albert G. Leep, "Social Studies
for Disadvantaged Youth, " Education (November-December
1971), pp. 85-91. Reprinted by permission of the authors
and publisher.

for and spending of available grants, and vociferous discussion in educational circles in the past few years, when the dust has settled one is forced to concur with Deutsch that "there is little overall curriculum planning for the needs of disadvantaged children."[2] However, on the positive side, an inspection of the educational literature would indicate that the hustle of recent activity in sponsoring education for disadvantaged children, scantily planned as it has been, has provided some important information and guide-lines by which educators may more effectively begin to assemble sequentially organized educational programs for disadvantaged children.

One of the important products of recent activities has been a more concise description of the value systems and resultant behavioral characteristics likely to emerge from the environmental milieu associated with poverty. Although it would be naive to assume that all children from economically deprived backgrounds exhibit equally all the characteristics associated with poverty, research findings indicate that the following characteristics are found frequently enough to be considered of primary importance in planning educational experiences to fit the needs and desires of this population. These characteristics are:

1. Whatever his racial background, one can be certain that the disadvantaged child is poor and this can be seen in the clothes he wears, his lack of a balanced diet, and his tendency to mistrust the typical adult. The home is usually characterized by: a lack of privacy, overcrowding conditions, and much noise or stimulation that lacks variety or meaning.[3]

2. The disadvantaged youngster has experienced no logical pattern in his life; things just happen.[4] The child lives for the present, the here-and-now, not for the future. He sees what his dilemma is and he wants it changed immediately. This can be seen by the fact that he has had little or no experience in setting and proceeding toward goals or in evaluating or reviewing past actions.[5]

3. Another important aspect of the child is that he possesses a negative self-concept.[6] More than likely, his early experiences have been extremely limited because of either lack of parental supervision or excessive control. He, therefore, does not see himself as a worthwhile, loved, or wanted individual.

4. The child is weak in communication skills--there is a lack of educational success in his language development. [7] The child tends to speak with just one word sentences, or phrases, or even incomplete thoughts. This is in complete contrast to the language structure of the majority of society.

5. The disadvantaged child possesses a set of values, many of which are in conflict with the prevailing value system of the school. [8]

6. The disadvantaged child lacks an adequate experiential development in comparison to middle class children. [9] Because these children are severely limited in their experiential backgrounds they do not have the opportunity to explore and to learn about their environment as well as others' environment.

7. The disadvantaged child has a deficiency in reading ability. [10]

8. The disadvantaged child lacks adequate or appropriate adult identification figures. [11]

9. The disadvantaged child places his emphasis upon the physical-motor coordination rather than the abstract. [12] Experiences are limited to action experiences rather than intellectual experiences.

With this brief overview of the characteristics generally found among large portions of our youth, let us now explore the considerations which are necessary in the planning of social studies programs for disadvantaged youth in the elementary school.

Social studies, of all the curricular areas, is the one which has been the least discussed and moved by the initiation of innovative programs for the disadvantaged. The reasons for the lethargy are not readily apparent, but the urgent need for attention in this area is intensified when one considers that social studies, as a study of man interacting with his social and physical environments, has much to offer to the alleviation of the "disadvantaged syndrome." Furthermore, this society has much to lose if the values and behaviors associated with poverty fail to be modified by an instructional program.

It is pertinent that we first examine the nature of existing social studies programs to discern those elements that prevent optimum learning of skills, attitudes, and concepts by disadvantaged students. Perhaps this examination of current "weaknesses" can best be made by enumerating those limitations of social studies programs most frequently cited.

The content of social studies programs: (1) is poorly organized sequentially in terms of developing ideas, skills and attitudes from level to level; (2) is primarily drawn from history and geography; (3) places emphasis on brief surveys of individual countries which tends to perpetuate stereotype views of other cultures and; (4) focuses a disproportionate amount of attention to the past, rural life and problem areas unrelated to the daily experiences of children.

Instruction in social studies tends: (1) to be textbook bound with emphasis upon reading and reciting; (2) to stress rote memory of facts, and; (3) to steer away from the examination of values and inquiry into social issues.

It suffices to indicate that the limitations of social studies programs have a deterring influence on the potential achievement of all students whether they be disadvantaged or not. However, of all students, the disadvantaged are least able to overcome the "weaknesses" cited above because their needs, concerns, background experiences, and motivational and learning techniques are least complemented by the content selected and the instructional devices used in existing social studies programs. Therefore, one of the major concerns of educators in planning programs becomes that of patterning the "how," "what," and "when" of instruction to more closely fit disadvantaged youth.

"To fit" does not imply that the overall objectives of social studies need to be compromised or that the school experiences of children should be confined to that which is simple, commonplace and conformity-oriented. Disadvantaged children do have certain characteristics--these were learned and can also be unlearned. Both the programs of instruction which condescend to and those which ignore the realities of the disadvantaged sell these students short educationally.

To attempt "to fit" does mean that realistic answers to the following types of questions are honestly sought in the planning and supplementing of social studies programs for disadvantaged youth.

1. Is the planning and development of the social studies
    curriculum based on the theory of participatory democ-
    racy?

    Many of the complaints about the various social and
political institutions have been lodged by the disadvantaged
because of a lack of cooperative decision-making. Too many
elements of our society have been planned and implemented
without consulting the people that will be most effected by
these grandiose decisions. The person segregated from the
total culture demands his share of the decisions, especially
if these decisions will affect his existence. The school can
add much more to its curriculum and its effectiveness if it
will draw upon many community resources, such as: parents,
students, and community leaders. These people can add much
to the planning, implementing, and evaluation of the social
studies curriculum. Furthermore, the people involved, as
well as the community, will achieve a feeling of pride and
self-esteem in that they were: consulted, took part in the
decision-making process, and were better able to understand
what the school was trying to accomplish for their children.
These community resources, in other words, were given the
opportunity to take part in fulfilling the goals of the parents
as well as the school.

2. Is the curricular plan built upon the assumption that the
    disadvantaged child brings many past experiences to the
    school?

    Many social studies programs emphasize the learning
of historical facts without relating these facts to the child's
past experiences. The disadvantaged child brings to the
school many positive as well as negative characteristics and
experiences and it is the duty of the school to either alter or
build upon these experiences. Too often, the school would
rather ignore the child's past and operate as if all children
are reared according to middle class practices. The social
studies program has much to lend in the growth of the child's
cultural and environmental background. In addition, the curriculum must take into account the child's interests. It would
appear that learning would be aided when the child's past experiences, interests, and the needs which derive from these
were satisfied in the classroom in some degree or form.

3. Is the curriculum plan built on the assumption that

disadvantaged youth bring to the classroom a background
of negative preschool and extra-school social studies
experiences?

Unlike the typical middle class child, the experiential
background of the disadvantaged has not prepared him to
view the various "community helpers" as helpers. Consequently, room must be made in the instructional plan for his
viewpoints and experiences; otherwise, the discrepancies between the cognitive and affective nature of his experiences
and those of the materials presented will curtail his true
involvement in the instructional activities.

4. Is the social studies curriculum built upon a functional
    approach in the understanding of the social, political,
    and economic forces of the disadvantaged child's environ-
    ment?

By functional is meant an approach that a child can
use immediately in his environment and has transfer value
in his future existence. This child needs to learn how to
live in an urban society. Perhaps a study, in depth, of the
many community problems, such as: housing, sanitation,
employment, recreation, pollution, etc., can be of service
to this child. Social studies for the disadvantaged child
should deal with an examination of the social, political, and
economic forces which rule as well as stifle his existence
and creativity. An examination of these forces and providing
of alternative solutions to these problems can be most useful
to these students. Much of this information is familiar to
this child for he is constantly bombarded with these forces.
As time is taken to: examine these forces, inquire about
alternative decisions, look at a means for social change, and
view the inconsistencies of a modern society, children are
developing inquiry skills which are vital to a responsible
citizenry in a rapidly changing society.

5. Are the experiences provided emphasizing the sequential
    development of social studies skills which become the
    fundamental tools for continued learning?

A unique type of social education is needed for the
disadvantaged child: one which helps him to analyze the
phenomena occurring in his environment and the social problems involved. Such an endeavor requires the ability to
locate, categorize, and weigh information in order that de-
ductions can be made, alternatives viewed, and predictions

of likely outcomes formulated. This type of instruction, which will foster the growth of these skills, can potentially replace the child's feelings of helplessness in coping with his rapidly changing world. This can be accomplished by acquainting the student with the tools, skills, and attitudes essential in producing political and social progress.

6. Is the content selected man-centered?

Disadvantaged children have a perceptive understanding of people and can comprehend the social, political, and economic forces when these forces and concepts are presented in a functional manner related to the activities of human beings. Furthermore, the study of people rather than solely institutions provides the identification figures by which disadvantaged children may measure the elements of their own lives, tie themselves and their families to the cultural heritage of America, and find worthy models to emulate.

7. Is there a multitude of educational materials and activities and do these compensate for verbal and social handicaps?

Joyce, [13] in a discussion of Hunt's[14] research, suggests that one of the primary needs of the disadvantaged child is a supportive, friendly relationship with people in situations requiring the communication of ideas, joint decision making and the general "give-and-take" by which the child may learn about groups as well as to develop his facility in verbal communication. A multi-media approach emphasizing the desirability of active, concrete experiences can supplement the restricted physical and intellectual world of these children and thereby provide the backlog of sensory experiences necessary for understanding and using social studies concepts and skills.

8. Are the daily teaching objectives clearly defined behaviorally and the instructional methods simply structured?

Frequent evidence of progress and assurance of success is vital in sustaining the interest and effort of the disadvantaged child. The child's limitations for planning a procedure for the achievement of projected goals coupled with his negative self-concept, require that lessons be structured in such a manner that the goals and procedures necessary for achieving the desired ends are clearly developed and defined behaviorally and that progress made toward these objectives is discernible to the students. Otherwise the child

may be overwhelmed by the, seemingly, complexity of the
lesson, lose sight of goals which are far removed from the
immediate activities, and, subsequently, give up.

9. Does the social studies curriculum take into account
    the reading difficulties of the disadvantaged youngster?

Much of the material in the social studies deals with
reading: the reading of textbooks as well as the reading of
biographies and critiques of historical, economic, or social
significance. As stated previously, the disadvantaged child
usually is from two to three years deficient in his ability to
read and comprehend material given to him. Therefore, the
social studies must provide a variety of reference materials
for this child in order that the understanding of concepts can
take place. In addition, each social studies teacher of the
disadvantaged should be skilled in the understanding of the
reading process. The teacher must have a mastery of the
skills necessary in the reading of the social studies. Reading
for these children should not be a separate course but take
place in all aspects of the curriculum, especially social
studies for much of the understanding of social phenomena
takes place through reading. Teachers must thus take time
with children in helping them to read and how to read for
understanding in the social studies.

10. Does the social studies curriculum provide for a study
     of the contribution of minority groups?

It can easily be stated that children and teachers are
quite ignorant about ethnic culture and the contributions that
minority groups have made in the building of America. Most
social studies textbooks do not touch upon this area out of
pressure from: certain geographical sections of America,
certain individual lobbyists, and out of sheer ignorance about
this hidden heritage and culture. Through dealing with the
topic throughout the social studies, with candor and frankness,
it may provide: models for students to admire, knowledge
of contributions, heretofore, missing from textbooks, an up-
lifting of the self-esteem of these minority groups, and a
bridge for further communication between groups.

11. Is there a place in the social studies curriculum to deal
     with controversial issues--issues that effect the child's
     everyday life?

From past experiences, teaching and working with these

children, it has been found by the authors that the disadvantaged child is very atuned to the various forces, groups, and phenomena that effect his life. One of the characteristics of this child is that he is oriented to the present, here-and-now world. If this be true, the social studies needs to deal with current issues: issues that are usually swept under the rug as if they did not exist or at least not for the school's undertaking. Topics such as: race relations, the political powers in the community, the draft, the changing values of the generations, an examination of the social and economic realities of urban life, an examination of governmental philosophies, and many other issues that affect either the local community or the nation. Through this process, students can look critically at these problems, use the tools of analysis and objectivity in their examinations. Perhaps proposals for solutions may even be suggested and tested as to their effectiveness. Thus the social studies becomes an active, dynamic, and pragmatic influence in the child's life.

12. Does the social studies curriculum deal with the world of work in any respect?

It has been found in a number of studies that children from minority groups, when asked what occupation they would like to enter, responded in two ways: they either chose the sports or entertainment fields or they did not respond. It seems apparent that those students who did respond chose the sports or entertainment fields because, traditionally, these were the only areas open to people of minority groups. However, the aspect that is so frightening is the fact that most of these students had no idea of what they would like to do with their future. Perhaps the fault here lies with the school for if we assume that the school prepares students for their future in the world, then necessarily, the school must prepare students for the world of work. Since the social studies delves into most areas of the world of work, it seems indicative that the social studies should work in this area from the time the child enters the school. This can be done incidentally as well as through formal units. An approach such as this can acquaint the disadvantaged child with: the various areas of work, the requirements necessary for attainment, and an impetus for certain directions and goals.

13. Is there a place in the development or in the teaching of social studies for in-service education of teachers?

Overarching and permeating all efforts to provide an

effective social studies program for disadvantaged youth must
be the sincere desire of teachers to adapt instruction to the
needs of children rather than adapt children to the needs of
a program. Therefore, some type of education is necessary
for teachers who plan to teach in areas classified as disadvantaged. This in-service education must deal with the psychology of the disadvantaged child and the implications derived
that become applicable to the social studies. Without some
type of pre-service or in-service education, any attempts to
deal with such questions or criteria, as those provided, will
constitute a waste of time because the answers found will be
decidedly predetermined. The important variable is, thus,
teacher behavior--without the proper attitude, outlook, skill,
understanding, or rapport, no matter how grand the designs
may be, the program will never reach the heights expected.

It is apparent that elementary social studies can become a vital force in meeting the immediate and future needs
of disadvantaged children. However, to achieve this potential,
modifications and revisions must occur in programs, materials
and instructional approaches as traditionally conceived and, at
present, widely utilized. By coming to grips with the questions contained herein, it is possible that the social studies
curriculum can be reconstructed in forms which more adequately fit the needs, interests and work-ways of disadvantaged
children.

Notes

1. Robert Isenberg, "The Rural Disadvantaged," NEA
    Journal, LII (April, 1963), p. 27.

2. Martin Deutsch, "Some Psychosocial Aspects of Learning
    in the Disadvantaged," Teacher's College Record,
    LXVII (January, 1966), p. 263.

3. John Morlan and Robert Ramonda, "The Disadvantaged
    Child and his Culture," Teaching the Disadvantaged
    Child, Sidney Tiedt, editor (New York: Oxford
    University Press, 1968), p. 5.

4. John Gothberg, "Use of the Daily Newspaper to Teach the
    Culturally Disadvantaged About Government," Journal
    of Secondary Education, XLIII (October, 1968), pp.
    270-74; and Joseph Loretan and Shelly Umans, Teaching
    the Disadvantaged (New York: Columbia University Press,
    1966), p. 4.

5. Loretan and Umans, op. cit.

6. Dan Boney, "Some Dynamics of Disadvantaged Students in Learning Situations," Journal of Negro Education, XXXVI (January, 1967), p. 315-19.

7. Richard Arnold, "Social Studies for the Culturally and Linguistically Different Learner," Social Education, XXXIII (January, 1969), p. 73-76; and Martin Deutsch, "The Disadvantaged Child and the Learning Process," Education in Depressed Areas, A. Harry Passon, editor (New York: Columbia University Press, 1963), pp. 163-79.

8. Joseph Lohman, "Expose--Don't Impose," Reading for Social Studies in Elementary Education, John Jarolimek and Huber Walsh, editors (London: Macmillan Company, 1969), p. 252; and Hyman Rodman, "The Lower-Class Value Stretch," Poverty in America: a book of readings, Louis Ferman, editor (Ann Arbor: University of Michigan Press, 1965), pp. 276-85.

9. Dorothy Bryan, "Education for the Culturally Deprived: Building on Pupil Experience," Social Education, XXXI (February, 1967), pp. 117-18.

10. Robert Ramonda, "Reading Instruction," Teaching the Disadvantaged, Sidney Tiedt, editor (New York: Oxford University Press, 1968), p. 87. .

11. Robert Harighurst and Thomas Moorefield, "The Nature and Needs of the Disadvantaged," The Sixty-sixth Yearbook of the National Society for the Study of Education, Paul Witty, editor (Chicago: University of Chicago Press, 1967), pp. 8-39.

12. R. D. Miller, et al., Inner Conflicts and Defenses (New York: Holt, Rinehart, and Winston, 1960), p. 24; and Robert Harighurst, "Who are the Socially Disadvantaged?" Readings for the Social Studies in Elementary Education, John Jarolimek and Huber Walsh, editors (London: Macmillan Company, 1969), p. 235.

13. Bruce Joyce, Strategies for Elementary Social Studies Education (Chicago: Research Associates Incorporated, 1965), pp. 265-66.

14. David Hunt, "A Conceptual Systems Change Model and
     Its Application to Education, " (unpublished paper,
     Syracuse University, 1964).

9. CAREER EDUCATION
IN THE ELEMENTARY SCHOOL

Anthony M. Deiulio and James M. Young

John Smith, a senior at Wilford High who has been taking vocational courses during the last two years, now finds he is deeply interested in becoming a veterinarian. He is told by several colleges, unsympathetic to John's nonacademic courses, that he is ineligible for college admission.

Larry Jones has always been told that he is going to college. Larry, a high school junior with an above-average intelligence, finds school to be a bore. His interest lies in the mechanical world of taking an engine apart and creating a new design.

Mary Larson, a 10-year-old in the fifth grade, only has a vague idea of what her father does for a living. She seldom thinks about occupations. When asked what she wants to be when she grows up, she echoes her girlfriends' usual reply, "I want to be a nurse or a secretary or something like that."

It has become a kind of upper-class ideal in this country for many boys and girls to put off thinking about a possible occupation until after they graduate from high school. By this time it is often too late to make up the necessary requirements to enter certain professions and college.

It is now being suggested by leading educators that our nation's students need to be more successfully guided toward personal fulfillment through effective career education pro - grams. The U.S. Office of Education suggests career educa-

Anthony M. Deiulio and James M. Young, "Career Education in the Elementary School, " Phi Delta Kappan (February 1973), pp. 378-380. Reprinted by permission of the authors and publisher.

tion as a systematic way to acquaint students with the world
of work during their elementary and junior high years, and
to prepare them during their high school and college years
to enter and advance in a career field carefully chosen from
among many.

Presently, eight out of every 10 American students
are enrolled in either a college prep or a general education
curriculum designed to prepare them for college. Only two
of these eight students will ever obtain a baccalaureat degree.
Consequently, eight out of 10 students in this country are being
prepared to do what in fact six of them will not do. It is
being suggested that a comprehensive K-12 career education
program, one that introduces every student to the world of
work and prepares him for a place in it, is vitally needed if
the United States is to continue a viable work force and
maintain a leading status on the world scene in terms of
competitive production.

Recent research has indicated that developmental
maturation, in terms of career education, really begins
during the first year of school, is an ongoing process throughout one's formal education, and even extends into his adult
life. Authorities on developmental guidance say that, first,
occupational choice is a developmental process and, second,
the process is largely irreversible. They also maintain that
since career development begins in childhood, occupational
experiences are as essential to elementary school children
as they are to high school and post-high school youth. All
experiences, as well as lack of experiences, influence career
development.

Schools all over the country are now beginning to design and implement career education programs on both the
elementary and secondary levels. The following description
of occupational education programs is a cross section of
prevalent career education programs now being implemented
in our nation's elementary schools.

Designs and Approaches

One of the most activity-oriented and revolutionary
career education programs now underway in an elementary
school is the T4C (Technology for Children) program now in
action in some New Jersey schools. The T4C program is
described as

...not really vocational education in the familiar
sense of the word. It borrows heavily from vocational education, but then it also borrows heavily
from the British Infant School, and from the 'problem-solving' and 'hands-on' approaches to learning.[1]

In actual practice the elementary students study concepts in the academic area of language arts, science, math,
and social studies by engaging in the production of various
objects. For example, one group of fourth-graders actually
built a log cabin in their classroom when they were studying
Colonial American history. Another activity "included the
writing and staging of television programs in which the children are the authors, set builders, costume makers, camera-
men, directors, and critics."[2] One group of fifth-graders
studied a unit on aerospace by building a radio-controlled
airplane.

Some other school communities, like the Cobb County
Public Schools in Georgia, are designing life-centered, ac-
tivity-unit career education programs, and are now working
these units into the regular curriculum. Career specialists
work with K-6 teachers to plan and design these units, pro-
cure materials, contact resource personnel, and assist in the
actual implementation of the varied unit programs.

Concrete objectives pertaining to career development
are an integral part of every career education unit that is
developed. For example, Cobb County's Career Development
Program's theme includes: 1) the student's evaluation of
self-characteristics, 2) exploration of broad occupational
areas, 3) introduction to the economics and social value of
work, 4) introduction to the psychological and sociological
meaning of work, 5) exploration of educational avenues, and
6) development of the student's progress of decision making
based upon the foregoing items.[3]

Besides the integration of these six objectives in each
unit, the planners also developed six elements or components
to be incorporated into all units. The elements are: 1)
hands-on activities, 2) role playing, 3) field trips into the
community, 4) resource people into the classroom, 5) subject matter tie-ins, and 6) introduction to occupations in the
community that are relevant to the unit.[4]

The Seattle elementary schools have an interesting

approach in their career education program. Besides using
the unit-center approach, they have different activity centers
relating to different occupations, built right in the rooms:

> Located in various parts of the room are a number
> of activity centers, each keyed to learning about
> different tools and crafts.

> A nearby sewing center contains large department
> store pattern books, dog-eared from use by fashion-
> conscious young ladies but still helpful in promoting
> the study of fractions required to determine the
> amount of materials to buy. There is also a typ-
> ing center and even a 'bank.'[5]

An excellent audio-video approach has been developed
in the Ellensburg, Washington, schools to present occupational
information to children in grades 4-6. Occupations have been
divided into five major job families and 13 subsystems:

> Each of the 13 subsystems is a sound-slide pre-
> sentation designed as a self-instructional device.
> The pupil works at his own pace and is individually
> responsible for learning at each stage of the system.

> The colored slides, all cartoon characterizations,
> depict the worker in his environment. Each slide
> focuses on the worker performing typical tasks of
> his occupation. Thus a skilled manual worker is
> shown repairing an airplane. A clerical worker may
> be shown typing a letter or operating a calculator.[6]

Some schools in Illinois are using a multimedia approach to present occupation information in the elementary
schools. Eastern Illinois University is developing and testing multimedia occupational packages for K-9 students. In
the participating Illinois schools utilizing these multimedia
packages one might find:

> First-graders viewing slides of an electrician at
> work, listening to tapes on the work of an electri-
> cian, and wiring up light bulbs and switches to get
> the feel of what an electrician does.

> Fourth-graders make study models of dentures by
> using the rubber molds, plaster-like materials, and
> other materials that dental assistants use.[7]

Fifth- and sixth-grade students in the Bemus Point
Central School District in New York are being provided with
opportunities to learn more about themselves and the world of
work through a community-oriented exploratory program.
More than 100 community businesses and services have
joined the school in providing opportunities for students to
actively explore the world of work.

Each sixth-grader has six opportunities and each
fifth-grader has three opportunities to visit occupations of
his choice. A student may visit different places each time
or may elect to return to one he felt particularly interesting.
The occupational visits are conducted in small groups of two
to four students, with numerous follow-up activities back at
the school to enhance the students' knowledge of occupations.

The programs and materials that have been described
are representative of the kind of career education experiences
being provided for many elementary students today. Other
career education programs and materials with unique features
are presently being developed.

A New Emphasis

It is being recognized in many schools that are designing and implementing career education programs that
most of the occupational experience-oriented activities can
and should be integrated into a school's regular curriculum.
Kenneth B. Hoyt, professor of education at the University of
Maryland and one of the well-known authorities on career
education, recently authored Career Education: What It Is
and How To Do It, the most complete discussion of the career
education concept available to date. At the 1972 American
Personnel and Guidance Association convention, Hoyt stated
that career education must be seen as representing only a
part of American education. He maintained that career education should be viewed as a concept to be integrated into the
total educational system in ways that enhance rather than de-
tract from all other worthy goals. Hoyt stated that career
education is going to be a new emphasis in our schools involving the bringing together of many parts, not the building
up of one part over the other.

It is essential that career education begin in the elementary school because it enhances a child's self-concept and
lays the groundwork for directly identifying with occupations

78   Learning and Teaching

later in high school. A major objective of elementary education in a comprehensive career education program should be to discover the talents and interests of each child and to demonstrate their relationship to the work world.

     Career education appears to be much more than one more ephemeral school fad. It is here to stay, and the curriculum will be much more relevant because of its inclusion.

Notes

1. Ian Elliot, "Occupational Orientation Means Work for You," Grade Teacher, April, 1971, p. 64.

2. Richard B. Harnack, "Implementation of the Technology for Children Project," American Vocational Association presentation, date unknown.

3. Joel Smith, project director, Synopsis, Cobb County Occupational and Career Development Program, 1970, p. 2.

4. Ibid., pp. 3, 4.

5. Vivian Hedrich, "Seattle's Concentration on Careers," American Education, July, 1971, pp. 13, 14.

6. Gerald Diminicc, "You and Work--An Instructional System for Children in Elementary School," American Vocational Journal, November, 1969, pp. 22, 23.

7. Marla Peterson, "Occupacs for Hands-On Learning," American Vocational Journal, January, 1972, pp. 40, 41.

10. SCIENCE, MATHEMATICS, AND PERCEPTUAL SKILLS
     AT THE ELEMENTARY SCHOOL LEVEL:
     AN INTERDISCIPLINARY APPROACH TO LEARNING
     BASED ON MANIPULATIVE MATERIALS

Ronald G. Good

Jean Piaget and numerous other researchers strongly emphasize the critical importance of personal exploratory contact with concrete objects in developing logical thought patterns in the elementary-school-age child. In the introduction to their book on Piaget's theory of intellectual development, (7) Ginsburg and Opper state:

> ... For these reasons a good school should encourage the child's activity, and his manipulation and exploration of objects. When the teacher tries to bypass this process by imparting knowledge in a verbal manner, the result is often superficial learning.... This principle [that learning occurs through the child's activity] suggests that the teacher's major task is to provide for the child a wide variety of potentially interesting materials on which he may act.

The typical elementary school curriculum in the United States is so heavily oriented toward verbal learning that children rarely work with objects as part of the planned curriculum. In such a situation, pupils who are disadvantaged from the verbal learning standpoint are the most seriously handicapped.

Ronald G. Good, "Science, Mathematics, and Perceptual Skills at the Elementary School Level: An Interdisciplinary Approach to Learning Based on Manipulative Materials," The Journal of Teacher Education (Winter 1972), pp. 471-475. Reprinted by permission of the author and publisher.

Problem and Rationale

Science educators have come to realize that having various science curricula available does not ensure any significant degree of implementation by the elementary school teacher. A major stumbling block to curriculum developers and coordinators is getting the equipment into the hands of the children.

Science, mathematics, and perceptual skills provide the most logical and potentially effective vehicle for helping the young child learn how to learn. The major unifying factor underlying these three content areas is the great extent to which manipulative materials can comprise the entire program. The fact that the processes involved need not rely on verbal skills for the curriculum content is of increasing importance, since the lack of verbal ability can cause many children to fail in school when traditional curricula are used. The science, mathematics, and perceptual skills project proposed here utilizes Piaget's concepts as a theoretical framework, while dealing with the very practical problem of implementation by classroom teachers.

Science, Mathematics, and Perceptual Skills

Developing logical thinking abilities in children should be the top priority of elementary school teachers. The only comprehensive theory of cognitive development has been offered by Jean Piaget, who has been conducting research studies in this area for half a century. There can be no doubt that he will have an increasing influence on decisions that determine curriculum and instruction, especially in areas where concrete objects are critical. Piaget (14) associates experiences in the use of manipulative materials with the development of logical processes in children:

> ... I believe that logic is not a derivative of language ... it is the total coordination of actions, actions of joining things together.... This is what logico-mathematical experience is.... It is an experience which is necessary before there can be [mental] operations. Once the [mental] operations have been attained this experience is no longer needed and the coordination of actions can take place by themselves in the form of deduction and construction for abstract structures.

Perhaps the nature of science, mathematics, and perceptual skills as used in this article needs to be clarified. The common intellectual process involved in each of the three areas can be identified as searching for patterns. Science, commonly defined by scientists and science educators as an active process of "searching for order and regularity in nature," is merely another way of saying the same thing. Although theory and research on the use of manipulative materials in mathematics education is still in its beginning phase, enough evidence already exists to suggest that interest and achievement are greater when objects are an integral part of the program. (4, 5, 8, 9, 11) Perceptual skills refer to abilities closely related to the process of searching for patterns. Sharpening one's perceptions to the patterns in nature and mathematics involves more than logico-mathematical thinking. Art and constructive design offer many possibilities for children to work with manipulative materials and engage in physical and intellectual activities related to this process.

Jerome Bruner, (2) the most prominent advocate of learning by discovery, also focuses on the importance of manipulative materials. His position has been analyzed by Shulman: (17)

... The general learning process described by Bruner occurs in the following manner: First, the child finds regularities in his manipulation of the materials that correspond with intuitive regularities he has already come to understand.... For Bruner, it is rarely something outside the learner that is discovered. Instead, the discovery involves an internal reorganization of previously known regularities of an encounter to which the learner has had to accommodate.

The interdisciplinary nature of the project proposed here is not based on the need to use mathematics in the sciences (3, 1, 10, 16) but rather on the natural place of manipulative objects in science, mathematics, and perceptual skills. Research studies related to cognitive development strongly suggest that the content of these areas, which is predominantly nonverbal-based, has more to offer in helping to develop children who are capable of logical independent thought.

Curriculum

Developing the ability to think in rational, logical ways, while at the same time fostering an independent, confident attitude toward learning, should be the guiding principle for curriculum and instruction. (13) Piaget's work and the research inspired by it leave little doubt that the significant learning of the logico-mathematical type occurring in children up to eleven or twelve years of age is a direct outgrowth of personal experience with concrete objects. What kind of curriculum can ensure this? Actually two interrelated programs must be implemented. The one considered first involves the actual curriculum intended for classroom use. Activities should be centered upon manipulative materials that relate closely to the searching-for-patterns theme in science, mathematics, and perceptual skills. The second program involves teacher education correlated with the type of materials-centered curriculum described above.

1. <u>Children's program</u>. Three guidelines should be followed:

   a. Manipulative materials will be a major part of each activity. Symbolic or verbal learning will evolve naturally out of personal interaction with such materials.

   b. A variety of activities will be possible for children who are interacting with any particular set of materials. Children bring different experiences and abilities to any given situation. It is unreasonable to expect children, who have varying cognitive abilities, to exhibit similar aptitude in understanding the patterns and relationships inherent in selected sets of materials.

   c. Activities should require a minimum of teacher structure after children receive equipment. An important criterion in the selection and development of sets of materials will be the extent to which they are appropriate for and consistent with the intellectual characteristics of the children. Some fairly general guidelines can be drawn from the research now available on cognitive development in designing opportunities for activities.

The nature and structure of science, mathematics, and perceptual skills development provide the content for activities; and the results of research on cognitive development, the input for sequencing and content. Piaget has established that children develop intellectual abilities in identifiable stages; the specific age level will vary from child to child but the same sequence of the stages seems to be invariant among all children. For example, the ability to establish one-to-one correspondence between sets of objects is required to deal at any level with set theory in mathematics. Comparing the characteristics of two sets of things includes the number of things involved. If a one-to-one correspondence is established by a five-year-old child using two sets of objects, he may not necessarily believe the correspondence is lasting; changing the physical arrangement of one of the sets of objects may destroy the correspondence as far as he is concerned. The necessity of lasting equivalence may not be a logical thing for the child until many months later. (13)

These two facts--that most five-year-olds can establish one-to-one correspondence but cannot conserve this equivalency upon spatial rearrangement and that children can differentiate between two- and three-dimensional objects of a topological nature before they can do the same with objects of a Euclidean nature--provide valuable directives for curriculum and instruction development. Piaget's work has indicated the importance of having children of kindergarten age deal with many different kinds of two- and three-dimensional objects. Reproducing such objects on paper is very valuable in helping the child develop his abilities in perceptual spatial arrangements, which are closely related to his development of logical thinking. (15)

2. Teacher preparation program. Changing the basic structure of the elementary school curriculum necessitates a corresponding change in the preparation of teachers. The present system requiring teacher education institutions to prepare a prospective elementary school teacher for competency in all phases of the school curriculum is patently absurd. At least two different kinds of teachers must be prepared. One would be responsible for the science-mathematics-art types of activities, where learning--predominantly nonverbal in nature--is essentially in the realm of logical-mathematical structures. The other would have responsibilities in the reading-language arts-social studies portion of the curriculum, where use of written materials, verbal interaction, filmed materials, and other verbal modes of instruction predominate.

Approximately one-half of the child's day would be spent interacting with manipulative materials and in essentially non-verbal activities. There would, of course, be open communication with peers and teachers at all times. Activity would be characterized generally by individual work, with small groups forming whenever children decided they were appropriate. The teacher's role would be to make certain sets of equipment available to the children and to interact with individuals and small groups. The materials used would provide most of the structure, with the teacher allowing the children to structure their own learning. The teacher would make use of probing questions and activities in interacting with individuals, making certain that such verbal interaction communicated acceptance of all lesson-related student behaviors.

Although many millions of dollars have gone into the development and distribution of elementary science curricula, very little has changed in the vast majority of classrooms. Materials remain unused in closets and central storage systems because teachers feel unable to deal with a materials-centered curriculum. A lack of understanding, even a fear, of science and mathematics prevents the prospective elementary teacher from seeing their great potential value for helping children develop probing, inquiring minds.

The preparation of teachers for classroom instruction centered upon manipulative materials requires the recruitment of persons who are interested in the approach and have a great deal of time to involve themselves in such experiences prior to professional certification. Teachers who are not confident in dealing with equipment in relatively unstructured learning situations are likely to establish a structured textbook approach in their classrooms. Recently an encouraging trend has been a change in the architecture of schools to reflect an attempt at increased flexibility in approaches to curricular change. The pod arrangement of classrooms opening to a central area offers ideal opportunities for the establishment of a learning activities center, where the elementary student could spend a significant part of his day dealing with manipulative materials representative of the nature of science, mathematics, and perceptual skills.

The suggestions offered in this article represent only an outline of the very significant changes required to provide for children the experiences stressed by Piaget as so crucial to the development of independent, creative, logical thinking. To implement successfully the project proposed here would

require the efforts of many people working together in all
its various phases.

Notes

1. Blanc, Sam S. "Mathematics in Elementary Science."
   The Arithmetic Teacher 14:636-40; December 1967.

2. Bruner, Jerome S. Toward a Theory of Instruction.
   Cambridge, Mass.: Harvard University Press, 1966.

3. D'Augustine, Charles H. "Reflections on the Courtship
   of Mathematics and Science." The Arithmetic Teacher
   14:645-59; December 1967.

4. Dienes, Z. P. "Some Basic Processes Involved in
   Mathematics Learning." Research in Mathematics
   Education. (Edited by J. M. Scandura.) Washington,
   D.C.: National Council of Teachers of Mathematics,
   National Education Association, 1967.

5. Dienes, Z. P. and Jeeves, M. A. Thinking in Structures.
   London, England: Hutchinson Educational Press, 1965.

6. Feynman, Richard P. "What Is Science?" Address
   given at fourteenth annual convention, National Science
   Teachers Association, 1966.

7. Ginsburg, Herbert and Opper, Sylvia. Piaget's Theory
   of Intellectual Development. Englewood Cliffs, N.J.:
   Prentice-Hall, 1969.

8. Hollis, L. Y. "A Study to Compare the Effects of
   Teaching First and Second Grade Mathematics by the
   Cuisenaire-Gattegno Method with a Traditional Method."
   School Science and Mathematics 65:683-87; November
   1965.

9. Lucow, W. H. "An Experiment with the Cuisenaire
   Method in Grade Three." American Educational
   Research Journal 1:59-67; May 1964.

10. Mayor, John R. "Science and Mathematics: 1970's--
    A Decade of Change." The Arithmetic Teacher
    17:293-97; April 1970.

11. Nasca, Donald. "Comparative Merits of a Manipulative
    Approach to Second-Grade Arithmetic." The Arith-
    metic Teacher 13:221-26; March 1966.

12. National Education Association, Educational Policies
    Commission. The Central Purpose of American Edu-
    cation. Washington, D.C.: the Commission, 1961.

13. Piaget, Jean. The Child's Conception of Number. New
    York: W. W. Norton, 1965.

14. Piaget, Jean. "Development and Learning." Journal
    of Research in Science Teaching 2:176-86; 1964.

15. Piaget, Jean and Inhelder, Barbel. The Child's Con-
    ception of Space. New York: W. W. Norton, 1967.

16. Rosenbloom, Paul C. "Science and New Math." The
    Instructor 75:25ff.; October 1965.

17. Shulman, Lee S. "Psychological Controversies in the
    Teaching of Science and Mathematics." The Science
    Teacher 35:34-38; September 1968.

18. Sigel, Irving E. and Hooper, Frank H. Logical
    Thinking in Children: Research Based on Piaget's
    Theory. New York: Holt, Rinehart and Winston,
    1968.

11. BLACK CHILDREN AND READING:
WHAT TEACHERS NEED TO KNOW

Kenneth R. Johnson and Herbert D. Simons

If I could get my hands on my first-grade teacher
now, I'd break her chalk.

A commercial education institute which promises to
teach reading to people who failed to learn how in school is
running an ad with this caption. In the ad a forlorn young
girl peers at a pile of books she is not able to read. The
girl in the picture is white. If she had been black her statement about her first-grade teacher might have suggested a
broken neck, because of the greater failure of black students
in learning to read.

Why is the failure of black students greater? Teachers
are both ill-prepared and perhaps unwilling to move in directions which could make the difference between the success and
failure of their black students. In this article three suggestions are made both for initial teacher training and for in-
service training for teachers presently in the schools. First,
they must study black culture with an eye toward sympathetic
recognition of it as a legitimate minority culture; second, if
they are to teach reading, especially to poor black children,
they must understand black dialect; third, once they understand
black culture and black dialect, they must adapt their teaching
strategies accordingly.

Understanding Black Culture

"Change the child or change the curriculum" is at once

Kenneth R. Johnson and Herbert D. Simons, "Black Children
and Reading: What Teachers Need to Know, " Phi Delta Kappan
(January 1972), pp. 288-290. Reprinted by permission of the
authors and publisher.

a basic tenet and a cliché of American education. Most educators agree on the latter alternative and feel that they follow it. But this is not the case in the education of black children. How can a curriculum be tailored to the needs of these children when the teachers and curriculum writers know little about or simply disdain black culture? Educators who view black culture as a sick white culture are hardly qualified to make useful curriculum changes.

In their failure to recognize that black children are different, not inferior, American teachers have not been alone. It is a societal problem, but how can it be rectified? Toward this end we suggest a thorough steeping in black culture. Consider for a moment the value to a white teacher of this knowledge. In the black culture the relationship between a child and an adult differs from that in the dominant culture. The black child is not expected to carry on a discussion with an adult as if he or she were an equal, or an almost equal, with the adult. A teacher from the dominant culture whose criteria have been set by her experience with children from the dominant culture expects a conversational skill from the black child that is simply outside of his lifestyle. The teacher then often judges the child dull purely because he lacks a knowledge of the child's culture.

Another important difference is that many black children, particularly poor ones, are members of extended families. Often grandmothers, aunts, uncles, and cousins live under one roof. The small nuclear family characteristic of the white middle class is not their concept of a family. In addition, many reports have pointed out the disproportionate number of black families headed by females. This is partially a result of economic racism but, whatever its cause, it has produced a matriarchal cultural pattern which means that many black children think of a family as a mother, a grandmother, and children. Incidentally, if the family is economically sound, it can be a good family; a male head does not automatically mean that a family is as good as the literature would have one believe.

A black child from such an extended family will have difficulty identifying with the nuclear white family of the basal reader. He would be better served by beginning reading literature which honored and reflected his history rather than patently rejecting it.

One of the stereotypes many whites have of black people

is that blacks have more so-called natural rhythm. Black
people as a group do have more rhythm and the reason for
this is not genetic but cultural.   Dancing and participating in
musical activities is an integral part and much more emphasized in the black culture (compare a black church service
with a white one). Again, knowledge of the culture could aid
the student and the teacher.   More rhythmic activities should
be incorporated in teaching black children--for instance, putting multiplication tables to music and dance patterns.

Another cultural pattern that is somewhat different in
black culture is nonverbal behavior.   In many ways, black
people communicate differently with their body movements.
For example, black children can communicate anger, hostili-
ty, and rejection with their eyes.   The movement--shifting
the eyes away from another person in a quick low arc with
the eyes partly closed--is called "rolling the eyes."   The
most aggressive stance a black female can take is to place
one hand on the hip with one foot in back of the other and the
weight shifted to the back foot.   A slow fluid walk with the
head slightly raised and one hand either hanging limply or
tucked partly in a pocket is a sure sign that a black male is
defiantly walking away from an authority figure after a conflict situation.   This kind of information can be extremely
valuable to teachers who work with black children.

These are but a few characteristics of the black
culture, but they clearly make the point. Teachers of black
children must understand the culture of these children if
they expect success. Perhaps the reading readiness of the
black children should be determined by criteria from their
own culture.

Understanding Black Dialect

Many teachers believe that one variety of English is
correct, hence best. This variety is the one that teachers
think they speak and is the one taught in school.   Linguists
have labeled it standard English.

Many black children, however, speak a variety of
English linguists have labeled black dialect, black English, or
nonstandard Negro dialect.   Black dialect differs somewhat
from standard English in its phonology and grammar.   If teachers are to work effectively with black children who speak this
dialect, they must understand: 1) that black dialect is a

legitimate linguistic system; 2) that standard English is not
"better" than black dialect; and 3) that black dialect is systematic.

Black dialect is a legitimate linguistic system. Many
black people use it exclusively, while others use both standard
English and black dialect. The social situation and audience
determine which dialect or variety of English is used. Therefore correctness is a relative term. Standard English is not
correct if the audience has more difficulty in understanding
it than in understanding black dialect. Furthermore, language,
in this case black dialect, is an identity label; it is an index
or reflection of the speaker's culture. When teachers reject
black dialect or look on it as an illegitimate or inferior variety of English, they reject part of the identity of the person
who speaks it.

Black dialect is systematic. That is, it is not a collection of sloppy, random, erroneous sounds and grammatical
structures which the speaker carelessly utters. Instead, when
the phonological and grammatical deviations from standard
English heard in the speech of many blacks are contrasted
with the points in standard English, it is clear that these
deviations are consistent and systematic. Black people are
not making just any noises, but particular noises.

For example, there are certain phonological rules in
black dialect and particular sounds that are systematically
substituted where particular standard English sounds occur.[1]
One of the phonological rules can be summarized as follows:
If a word ends in two consonant sounds and both of them are
either voiced or voiceless, and the last consonant sound is
/b/, /d/, /k/, /p/, or /t/, then the last consonant is
reduced or omitted. Some words ending in two consonant
sounds conforming to the above rule are test, desk, lift,
and expect. These end in voiceless pairs of consonants, and
black children will pronounce them tes, des, lif, and expec.
The words told, mind, killed, and lived end in voiced pairs
of consonants; black children will consistently pronounce them
tol, mine, kill, and live. Teachers often note that black
children leave off the endings of words. They'd be able to
better instruct black children if they knew which endings
and the linguistic environments where the leaving-off occurs.

There are other examples of phonological deviations
from standard English that really comprise the system of
black dialect, and teachers can discover these when they quit

looking at black dialect as a collection of mispronunciations
and note the system, consistency, and frequency of these
deviations in the speech of black children.

The same phenomenon of system occurs in grammar.
The grammatical deviations black children make are not random. For example, the copula (is, am, are) is systematically omitted in present progressive tense (He looking at
me); the plural ending is often omitted if another word in the
sentence indicates pluralization (She have two brother); the
verb been is used to indicate distant past action (He been left
for home); this agreement-sound on the end of third person,
present tense verbs is omitted (He walk home). Linguists
have pointed out, by the way, that the verb system of black
dialect in some cases can indicate duration or time of action
more precisely than standard English.

Black Dialect and Teaching Reading

In recent years heated debate has raged about the
relationship between black dialect and learning to read.
Teachers should be aware of and keep up with the findings
and suggestions coming from the research generated by the
debate.

First, it is important for teachers to understand the
nature of the conflict that arises when a child's language is
rejected either explicitly or implicitly by his teachers. They
must understand the devastating emotional and social consequences of such an act, which the child views as a rejection
of himself and his culture. The negative impact upon motivation and progress in learning to read is serious. [2]

The frustration of having one's language rejected
would be clear to teachers if they themselves experienced
the rejection the black child goes through in school. Imagine
a teacher training class conducted by a black teacher who will
only tolerate black dialect. Every time the "students" lapse
into standard English, the black teacher admonishes and
corrects them for errors or stupidity. The teachers would
soon experience the torture of rejection and the difficulty of
changing one's dialect.

Second, teachers must become aware of specific conflict points between black dialect and standard English. This
knowledge will enable them to make the very important distinc-

tion between reading errors which must be corrected and pronunciation differences which are dialectic, hence are not errors
and can therefore in many cases be safely ignored. For
example, teachers can stop confusing and frustrating black
children by telling them that pin and pen have different
vowel sounds. In black dialect they both have the same
vowel sound. And when a black child reads "tol" for "told"
the teacher should not correct him, since he has not made a
reading error. On the other hand, when the child reads
"pass" for "passed" or "like" for "liked," he may or may
not know that the past tense has been signaled.[3] Here the
teacher must determine from the larger sentence or para-
graph context or from diagnostic tests whether or not the
child needs to learn that the "ed" is a past tense marker.

Again, these are just a few examples; but they serve
to give the teacher a sense of the significance for teaching
of a knowledge of the phonological conflict points. Teachers
should further be aware that synthetic or blending phonics
methods also may create problems, because they exaggerate
the conflict points and therefore must be tailored to ghetto
teaching. This is not a suggestion to abandon phonics--just
a reminder that it must be adjusted to avoid conflict points,
as many teachers now do to compensate for regional dialect
difference. As a general rule children should be allowed to
impose their phonological systems on standard English
spellings.

Grammatical conflict points must be clear in the
minds of teachers also. The deletion of the copula in black
dialect mentioned earlier is a good example of this. Teachers'
sensitivity to this area of conflict will prevent many comprehension difficulties.

At present there are three major curriculum proposals for handling grammatical conflict points. The first
is to delay reading until the child learns to speak standard
English grammar or to teach standard English concurrently
with reading. The second is to allow dialect reading of
standard English texts. The third and most radical suggestion is to translate beginning reading texts into black dialect.[4]

Teachers are already aware of the problems inherent
in the first approach. Until now they have tried to change
the dialect of these children and have failed. It is almost
impossible to change dialect in school, since children get
their dialect from peer groups. Only massive integration

would make this a feasible alternative--and massive integration is not imminent.

The second proposal, allowing dialect reading of standard English texts, seems a sensible first step in line with current knowledge. Essentially, the child would be translating standard English into his own dialect. Using this method, for example, the teacher would allow the child to read "He going" for "He is going" as long as it didn't interfere with his comprehension. In order to implement this proposal teachers must have, as mentioned previously, a working knowledge of black dialect and where it conflicts with standard English.

The third proposal, which involves writing at least the beginning readers in dialect, is based on two assumptions. First, children will learn to read better from materials written in their own language. Second, books written in dialect will eliminate the need for the child to translate into his own dialect. This extra translating, it is suggested, interferes with comprehension. Whether or not these assumptions are correct and thus justify the use of dialect readers is not yet known.

Much more research needs to be done on these alternatives before there can be any definitive answers. In the meantime it is important for teachers to remain flexible and to be willing to try these new ideas. What is quite clear is that we are now failing miserably to teach black children to read, and there is no justification for maintaining the status quo.

To summarize, teachers need much more knowledge of black culture. They need to know black dialect, its conflict points with standard English, and how to handle these conflicts in teaching reading. This knowledge and its application in the classroom will provide a first step in improving the reading skills of black children. There is no excuse for allowing a teacher's ignorance of his student's culture and language to stand in the way of a child's learning to read.

Notes

1. Ralph W. Fasold and Walt Wolfram, "Some Linguistic Features of Negro Dialect," Teaching Standard English in the Inner City. Washington, D.C.: Center for

Applied Linguistics, 1970, pp. 41-86.

2. W. Labov and C. Robins, "A Note on the Relation of
    Reading Failure to Peer Group Status," Teacher's
    College Record, 1969, pp. 395-406.

3. W. Labov, "The Reading of the -ed Suffix," in H. Levin
    and J. Williams (eds.), Basic Studies on Reading.
    New York: Basic Books, 1970.

4. W. Stewart, "On the Use of Negro Dialect in the Teach-
    ing of Reading," in J. Baratz and R. Shuy (eds.),
    Teaching Black Children to Read. Washington, D.C.:
    Center for Applied Linguistics, 1969.

12. AN ASSIGNMENT ON ECOLOGICAL AWARENESS

Thomas G. Vinci

Student teachers have been cloistered for many years in classrooms and libraries in our teacher training institutions. It is time to expose them to the environment that the pupils they are to teach come from. This is especially true for our teachers who plan to serve in an urban neighborhood. They have to understand the background which plays a very large part in pupils' attitudes toward learning.

One way of acquainting student teachers with the milieu of their pupils is to give them relevant assignments which have a practical approach to the various problems they will encounter as beginning teachers. In an urban teacher training institution especially, the offering of such creative, stimulating, and organic assignments is of paramount importance. These assignments should enable both the student teacher and his pupils to leave the classroom and to interact with the community, thus creating a viable and needed coordination of the pupils' two worlds.

An assignment could be given, for example, to research and develop proposals for the improvement of a neighborhood: to clear empty lots, parks and fields for recreational areas or to improve the appearance of buildings. This assignment would be part of a science module cluster. The student teacher would be expected to write proposals for the improvement of the environment immediately surrounding the school in which he observes and teaches. Through this assignment student teachers would involve pupils, cooperating teachers and parents; and others in the community could be made more aware of some means of improving the neighborhood through cooperative endeavors.

As a first step in such an assignment, the student teacher and the class would walk through the school neighbor-

---

Unpublished paper, included by permission of the author.

hood, familiarizing themselves with its various resources.
Some of their discoveries would probably include types of
vegetation, natural and man-made building materials, and
human resources. Next, the student teacher, aided by his
pupils, would begin writing proposals on topics such as the
following:

> Potholes--Let's Do Something About Them
> A Projected Plan to Help Improve the Park
> A Proposal for an Anti-Graffiti Program
> A Film Project--Celebrate Your Block
> A Community Mural
> A Ballfield in the Neighborhood
> Graffiti Art All Around Us
> Establishing a Safe Playground
> Establishing a Recreational Project for a
>   Housing Project
> A Pond on Our Street
> Outdoor Flowers and a Few Patches of Green

In their planning, the student teachers would be expected to include any educational implications arising naturally
from the implementation of the proposals. Thus, in addition to stating project goals, the student teacher would outline
ways in which the use of science, social studies, physical
education, art, mathematics, reading, and language arts
could be included. The student teacher would also develop
evaluation instruments.

Hopefully, the parents association and the community
school board might become interested in carrying out one or
several of the proposals submitted by the student teachers
and their pupils. What started out to be an assignment in a
methods course at the university could turn out to be a workable plan through which life in the school neighborhood might
be bettered.

Perhaps the ideas suggested here seem too idealistic
or too difficult for the student teacher to achieve. However,
when the suggestions were made to student teachers that they
develop a project in ecological awareness, they responded
with enthusiasm and confidence. Following in this report
are three examples of student teacher projects developed and
submitted through such an assignment.

Potholes--Let's Do Something About Them

The following is a proposal made to the children of my class about a serious problem which exists in the neighborhood of the school, namely, "potholes."

My first task was to take my class on a walk through the streets surrounding their school. I pointed out the first pothole we encountered. I asked my class to observe the pothole and its relationship to traffic for about ten minutes. My pupils reported the following observable cause and effect relationships:

1. Cars seem to go a little out of control after a wheel goes into a pothole.

2. The faster a car hits a pothole, the higher it jumps in the air.

3. Sometimes a driver seems to spot the pothole and slams on his brakes in order to avoid it. The result is that the car in back almost hits the car which brakes.

My class concluded that potholes in their streets are dangerous and unacceptable. Where did these potholes come from? How did they get there? These were the questions being asked of the teacher.

I explained that potholes are not mysterious; they are even predictable because they come about due to scientific relationships. I then set up a series of classroom experiments to explain how a nice, flat, paved street can become pockmarked with potholes.

Our first experiment was to take a small paper cup and fill it up to the rim with water. Each pupil then took his cup to the refrigerator in the teacher's cafeteria, where we placed the cups in the freezer compartment. After the water froze, my pupils examined their cups. Everyone knew the water would turn into ice, but not everyone knew that they would "get more ice than water," as one of my pupils reported. The ice was above the rim of the cup. We repeated the experiment many times, carefully marking the pre-freezing water levels in the various containers selected by the children. The children concluded that when water changes into ice, "it gets bigger and takes up more space."

Our next experiment was to discover the strength ex-
hibited by water as it changes from water to ice. Each
pupil carefully hollowed out a small ball of modeling clay.
A small hole was left on the surface through which water
was injected with water pistols. After each ball was completely filled, the small hole was sealed with a pellet of
clay. Then, the water-filled clay balls were placed in the
freezer. When they were taken out of the freezer, the children observed the condition of the balls. The children reported that "there were cracks in the shell with ice sticking
out." They concluded that as water changes into ice, it can
"push and move things," as it had the shell of the clay ball.

Using the new concepts my students had mastered, I
proceeded to set up a demonstration about how streets develop
potholes. Each pupil filled an empty cigar box with dirt and
small pebbles. We then placed a black plastic cover over
the dirt. (The cover represented the asphalt paving which
covers the soil under our streets. Incidentally, not every
student was aware that there is earth under the asphalt.) We
then painted yellow lines down the centers of the covers in
order to represent the dividing line for two-way traffic. Toy
cars were placed in traffic patterns on the "streets." I then
instructed my students to make some tiny holes on the surface of their plastic covers. Water was poured into the tiny
holes, and the simulated streets were placed in the freezer.
Upon removing our streets from the freezer, there was much
chaos. Cars had overturned. The streets had risen, in
some places as much as one inch above where it was before
being placed in the freezer. The streets were generally
lumpy, and nowhere near as smooth as they were prior to
freezing. My students were now telling their teacher how
potholes came to be.

One student was able to go a step further and conclude that potholes could only develop when the temperature
dipped to 32° or below. From this, he further concluded
that potholes should be in abundance during the winter.
Another student said that if it did not rain or snow, potholes
would not have a chance to develop, no matter how cold it
became.

I then explained how some potholes became trenches.
A pothole will grow larger and larger if there is a continual
pattern of freezing and thawing, combined with a plentiful

supply of snow and rain.

My class began proposing ideas of what they would do about potholes. The following were some of their ideas:

1. During the pothole season, December to March, maps could be distributed at gas stations, bicycle shops, and parking lots, which would show the location of potholes with depths of at least three inches.

2. Copies of our pothole maps could be sent to various newspapers, the Department of Highways, the Police Department, local legislators, and the borough president. Letters would be sent, along with the maps, requesting that the potholes be fixed.

By utilizing an observable occurrence in the children's neighborhood--potholes--the children were able to learn various scientific facts about the process of water changing to ice. Instead of learning these facts abstractly, the children were able to relate what was learned to a concrete situation. This was not only a help to learning, but also a strong motivating factor which got the children interested in scientific research. Another aspect of the project was that at the end, the children felt that they, perhaps, could help others by mapping the location of the potholes in their area.

A Community Mural

The east and west walls of our school are ugly. These walls certainly have a negative effect upon the children attending our school. Many local children have shown how they feel about these walls by filling a long stretch of them with graffiti. Perhaps, if the walls were not so empty, the neighborhood children would not feel compelled to vandalize them so.

We are proposing that the students of our school be allowed to use these two walls as a canvas to express their feelings about their community and environment. Theirs is a multi-ethnic area; so, we propose to paint these walls using the colors red, yellow, black and white to symbolize the four races who live in our community. To show that we realize that these different races can all add to the possible harmony of our environment, we will also use the color green for ecology.

By beautifying these ugly walls, we hope to make our
school a nicer place in which to learn. We are also undertaking this task to encourage and invite camaraderie and
amusement in the adjoining playground. Our aim is simply
to make our neighborhood a bit more livable.

We propose to have the students of our school paint
the bottom seven feet of these walls themselves. Each grade
level of the school, pre-K through 6, will be given a section
to work on. The children will submit possible murals using
"Brotherhood and Ecology" as a theme. Suitable material
will be picked for each grade level. These will be adapted
to the walls by the children of the school.

A commercial artist is to be employed to extend the
work done on the lower part to cover the entire wall.

Project Goals and Objectives

1. To beautify the neighborhood.
2. To encourage pride in the neighborhood.
3. To create a healthier learning environment for
    the school.
4. To encourage harmony in the playground so that
    play will be productive.
5. To foster attitudes of brotherhood in the neigh-
    borhood.
6. To nurture the concept that "people are a resource
    of our ecology. "
7. To use the project as a springboard to develop
    various aspects of school curriculum on all
    grade levels.

Some suggested applications are:

Science

1. Comparison of durability of different brands and
    kinds of paint used.
2. Discovery of how well various colors cover graffiti.
3. Study of effects of air pollution on mural over a
    time period.
4. Use of pulleys and scaffolding.
5. The blending of colors--study of light.
6. Research into the nature of paint and other
    materials of project.

Social Studies

1. Involvement in cooperative efforts and planning needed to organize and implement the project.
2. Stimulation of pride in community.
3. Development of non-verbal communication--art.
4. Study of the economics of funding.
5. Development of a unit on "the company" and need for public relations.
6. Understanding the themes of Brotherhood and Ecology.
7. Participation in discussions on:
   a. Why was the graffiti put on the walls?
   b. Will the mural be defaced with graffiti?
   c. What is a community?
   d. How has project affected the school?

Physical Education

1. Bringing class outdoors while working on project.
2. Increasing kind of meaningful physical exercise and muscle development (especially on the early childhood level).
3. Development of the concept and appreciation of "work."

Art

1. Poster campaigns.
   a. Learning how to create "wet paint" posters.
   b. Cooperating to discourage vandalism of murals.
   c. Growing through individual expression of the two themes.
2. Discussion about murals.
   a. Seeing the mural as an art form.
   b. Study of other wall murals in New York City.
   c. Artistically expressing of the themes of Brotherhood and Ecology.
3. Other art areas:
   a. Working with oils.
   b. Developing color coordination.
   c. Learning perspective.
   d. Learning spatial relationships.
   e. Experiencing harmony.

Mathematics

1. Increasing measurement skills.
2. Learning about addition and multiplication through computations of the area.
3. Learning estimation--surface area and coverage of paint.
4. Discovering elementary concepts of space and its allocation.
5. Setting up time schedules for working on project.
6. Practical math problems related to cost and funding.

Language Arts

1. Engaging in verbal communication within the class and between classes throughout the project.
2. Writing and developing the project itself.
3. Reading about history of murals--use of the newspaper as a source of information.
4. Researching paint and other materials.
5. Expanding vocabulary and concepts.
6. Keeping work sheets, schedules, and diaries about working on the project and its progress.
7. Developing creative expression through writing about what one's particular proposed mural means.

We have not delineated our curriculum area activities into particular grade levels because we want this project to include all the children in the school. It will then be the job of individual teachers (hopefully, motivated by the workshops) to make the most of this project. Teachers would be encouraged to incorporate whatever aspects of the project that are applicable to their classes and to make those applications in a manner suitable to the level of the class.

Plan of Action

1. Get in contact with the school administration for necessary permissions.
2. Get in contact with teachers and other faculty members to solicit their ideas and cooperation.
3. Get in contact with parents and other members of community to solicit their ideas and cooperation. (Letter to be mimeographed in English and Spanish).
4. Evaluate feedback from steps 2 and 3.

5. Devise initial correspondence to paint companies.
6. Evaluate reaction of paint companies. (If needed, get in contact with other paint companies.)
7. Engage commercial artist.
8. Initiate neighborhood publicity program--flyers, posters, letters to community groups, rallies, assemblies, class trips to other murals in city.
9. Begin to have children submit art work.
10. Elect class representatives to meet with commercial artist and choose final children's work for class murals.
11. Ask artist to submit ideas to children for approval.
12. Establish workshops and organizational meetings for teachers and the parents to schedule time and allocate spaces for murals.
13. Begin children's art work on murals.
14. Ask artist to begin work.
15. Upon completion of entire wall, declare "Brotherhood and Ecology Day" to be accompanied by a Saturday afternoon neighborhood picnic.
16. Continue periodic maintenance over the years.

A Pond On Our Block

I. Location:

Pond to be constructed on property measuring 45' x 60' between two buildings of a housing project on our block directly across from the public school. At present. the property is bare, with little grass growing and no trees.

II. Community Involvement:

This project is to be a community effort utilizing community support and manpower. To achieve this goal, the class will consult and invite to participate the following:

a. The local community center.
b. The public and parochial schools adjacent to the property.
c. Residents and administration of the housing project.
d. The parent associations of the schools.

It is hoped that a wide base of community support and involvement will provide the manpower needed for planning, construction, and maintenance. In addition, the project will be

a source of pride for the community and provide aesthetic
enjoyment.

III. Procedure:

       a. To determine the agency responsible for the prop-
erty involved so as to obtain permission for the project,
the class will get in contact with:

       1. New York City Environmental Protection Agency.
       2. New York City Parks Department.
       3. New York City Housing Authority.

In addition to seeking permission for the proposal, the above
class will investigate the agencies as possible sources of
financial and other assistance.

       b. To determine the cost of construction and to in-
vite donations, the class will send letters to community
nurseries and pet stores.

       c. To obtain funding for the project, the class will
organize fund raising campaigns.

IV. Educational Implications:

       It is assumed that the participants in this project
will be lacking a working knowledge of the factors involved
in constructing and maintaining an artificial pond. Therefore, the research necessary before construction begins is
taken as a vital aspect of the educational implications of the
proposal. The students will be presented with the problem
and will be given an opportunity to hypothesize about its solution and, finally, to research the problem and carry out
possible solutions.

       More specific educational implications are the following:

       A. Science

            1. Plant life
                a. Discovery of conditions necessary for
                    growth.
                b. Comparisons of different plants and their
                    rate of growth.
                c. Comparison of plants that grow in soil
                    with those that grow in water.

   2. Animal life
      a. Study of the life cycle of animals.
      b. Study of the necessary conditions for
         animal growth.
   3. Ecology (the interdependence of plants and
      animals).
   4. Weather (the effect of seasonal changes on
      plants and animals).

B. Art

   1. Initiation of poster campaigns for community
      support.
   2. Running an art sale as funding activity.
   3. Advertising for funding activities.
   4. Making paintings, drawings, murals, dioramas
      of the pond.

C. Language Arts

   1. Researching the project will provide reading
      experience and involvement in the following
      skill areas: library skills, using the ency-
      clopedia, outlining, finding the important facts.
   2. Reading for enjoyment about the life of the
      pond--prose and poetry.
   3. Viewing films and photographs about ponds.
   4. Written expression.
      a. Writing letters to city agencies, nurseries
         and pet stores.
      b. Writing thank you letters.
      c. Developing stories expressing feelings
         about the pond.
      d. Developing poetry expressing feelings
         about the pond.

D. Mathematics

   1. Arriving at construction costs.
   2. Examining funding campaigns.
   3. Charting the growth of plants and animals.
   4. Counting the number of plants and animals.

E. Social Studies

   1. Learning to work with various groups for a
      common goal.

    2.   Learning about community workers and how
they contribute to the community.

Other assignments that may lead student teachers and
their pupils to carry out projects for community improvement might include:

The Disposal of Waste Materials
Poor Safety Conditions on the Block and in the Neigh-
borhood
Adopting and Caring for a Curbside Tree
The Problem of Stray Dogs and Cats and What Can Be
Done About It
Erosion and Weathering of Soil and Rocks
Leaves--Where They Come from and Where They Go
Many Types of Changes Occurring in the School Envi-
ronment; e.g., Physical, Social, Economic and
Political
The Effects of Air and Water Pollution on the Neigh-
borhood.

The suggestion of at least some of these proposals in
methods courses would give most student teachers studying at
institutions located in an urban environment a way of teaching
through an interdisciplinary approach. This approach would
involve student teachers and their pupils in planning goals of
learning, carrying out actual projects, and evaluating project
outcomes within a meaningful framework. This approach
might increase school-community cooperation, an invaluable
asset to the learning atmosphere for teachers and their pupils.

13. ACCOUNTABILITY IN URBAN ELEMENTARY SCHOOLS

Barney M. Berlin

The notion of accountability is seductive. Even the most cursory examination of our urban schools reveals that there are many areas of instruction which have been less successful than expected. Parents whose children have spent years in school and are still virtually illiterate, and parents who read about the fine schools and excellent academic performance of suburban students are looking for a way of transforming their school to resemble the ideal. Administrators, feeling the pressure of an aroused public, are seeking a way of changing the school and distributing the pressure. After all, it can be argued, the administrators don't actually teach.

While it is true that the notion of accountability has also been adopted by both liberals and conservatives for differing reasons (8), it would be unfair to adopt the cynical conclusion that the move for accountability is primarily an attempt to gather power. Just as in other human endeavors, motivation in the area of accountability is determined by numerous factors, although I am convinced that the overriding desire of most advocates of accountability is to find a systematic approach which will cause the schools to improve in the direction espoused by each accountability advocate.

If one accepts the premise that our schools need improvement, and the notion that someone should be responsible for previous results and future improvement, there are two basic approaches to accountability (4). The first can be characterized as the "input-output" approach. One analyzes the educational goals and the factors involved in achievement of the goals, and determines the amount and kind of achievement to be expected, then holds someone responsible if the goals aren't reached.

Unpublished paper, included by permission of the author.

The second approach is typified by the "voucher plan." In this case, accountability comes from the public pressure on a school and its teachers which develops if parents can send their children to any school they choose. Of course, each parent judges the school by differing criteria, so that a school might have to project numerous images. Teachers who have taught in private schools are also aware that educational values are sometimes compromised in order to maintain enrollment and tuition at the necessary levels.

In the past three years, most of the emphasis has been on the first approach to accountability. This approach lends itself to development of models, such as those proposed by Barro (1) Dyer (3) and MacDonald and Forehand (6) in which one defines input and conditions, and hopefully develops a procedure for determining theoretical and real output.

The pitfalls of accountability have been pointed out by many authors (8). These pitfalls can be summarized in four categories:

1. Definition of Accountability

After everyone agrees that accountability means being held responsible, numerous questions arise which have no agreed-upon answer. For example, who is accountable? Who determines accountability? Are there consequences of accountability? The attempt to answer any of these questions could occupy a school board or local school council for months, without a satisfactory resolution of the question for all parties involved.

2. Defining Goals

Assuming a definition of accountability, the goals of education must be defined. Here we run into arguments over short-term versus long-term goals; behavioral objectives versus general objectives; omission of hard-to-define objectives in favor of inclusion of simple skills which are easily defined; and other similar questions not easy to resolve (including, how and by whom goals are to be defined).

3. Measurement of Achievement

After resolving all preceding questions we must now determine how to measure the achievement of the goals we have defined. Unfortunately, a new set of questions and doubts arises to plague us. Should we use norm or criterion-referenced tests? How do we compensate for the various defects which have been identified in the tests? What group of children do we compare with what control group or norm? How do we avoid the effects of teaching for tests? And finally, what does it mean to say that a class gained a certain amount in a specified time?

4. Assigning Responsibility

Let us assume our goals have been defined and achievement measured. Who takes credit for the achievement? (Many writers assume blame and accentuate the negative.) How is the credit divided? Is it sufficient for 30 out of 32 children to achieve adequately? Is the school the sole source of learning? How do we account for any changes observed?

Recognizing the objectives summarized above, the question of why professional educators should proceed to develop models of accountability naturally arises. Since so many problems occur when one tries to establish an accountability system, wouldn't we be better off without one? There seem to be two undeniable factors in the situation: the schools are not always successful with every child, (just as this is being written, the Chicago Sun-Times bears the headline "Report Shows Chicago Pupils Lag on National Tests"), and parents, community groups and administrators are demanding accountability from their schools. Thus, we seem to have little choice. We can develop an accountability system which we feel, as educators, provides maximum protection for the educative process; or, we can have an accountability system developed by outsiders and imposed on the educational system. As Ornstein and Talmage (7) state: "With accountability, the process of teaching and administration is deemphasized, and it is their effects upon student performance which is emphasized. In short, the attempt is to estimate the teacher's or administrator's ability to produce behavioral change in a group of students." Thus, it seems clear that we should explore possible accountability models and choose to experiment with some to enable us to produce a situation which is not counter-productive in terms of public demands on education and educators.

As we mentioned earlier, three models of accountability have been developed. The Barro (1) model concentrates on the role of the teacher, but includes numerous safe-

guards and structures which hopefully prevent the teacher
from becoming a martyr for accountability.

The Dyer model (3) emphasizes the teacher to some
extent, but also establishes a chain of accountability including
the administration of the school district. Both Dyer and
Barro include factors such as the nature of the community,
nature of the home, and characteristics of the learners in
the models. Dyer and McDonald and Forehand (6) attempt
to move the emphasis from the individual teacher and individual child to a collective school responsibility.

The McDonald-Forehand model, developed partially
on the basis of the New York City experience with community control, places heavy emphasis on community input, and
is cyclical. This model proposes an ongoing evaluation process (formative) with frequent adjustment as new data are
available.

In the development of any model, certain questions
must be answered. These include:

1. What results are we holding someone or some
   group accountable for?
2. What factors are to be considered as playing a
   role in the outcome of instruction (which is the
   product for which we hold people accountable)?
3. How do we evaluate the educational outcome?
4. What weight do we assign to various factors involved in the educational process (is the home
   15 or 25 %)?
5. What changes are to be made in the educational
   process, either resulting from formative or summative data?

As one answers the above questions and develops an
accountability system, it is well to include the safeguard
questions listed by Ornstein and Talmage (8, p. 79).

Does the proposed accountability plan:

1. Impose moderating restraints and regulating activities to prevent scapegoating of educators?
2. Define the relationships between lay people and
   educators?
3. Provide for the involvement of teachers and
   school administrators in all stages of development

and coordination of the plan?
4. Reflect the school district's philosophy of education?
5. Call for a careful pilot testing period prior to mass-scale implementation?
6. Allow for professional evaluation and self-evaluation?
7. Provide comparative data with similar schools for self-study and improvement?
8. Contain grievance and appeal procedures with adequate professional representation in cases where teachers and administrators are evaluated in terms of student performance?
9. Include equal employment opportunity for all educational personnel?
10. Protect personnel against intimidation from local groups and prevent favoritism toward one group?
11. Guard against the possible danger of pitting Human beings against each other, whether this involves students against students or teachers against teachers?
12. Have the support of state agencies in providing guides or data for professionals and lay people alike about test problems and errors of measurement scores?
13. Provide adequate time intervals between pre- and post-testing?
14. Take into consideration the multiplicity of variables associated with learning?
15. Include learning outcomes beyond narrowly defined behavioral objectives?

These questions, if raised properly, could prevent many of the conflicts which inevitably arise when one attempts to fix responsibility.

Accountability Model

The accountability model illustrated in Figure 1 can be summarized as: 1) Determination of goals on the basis of community, faculty, and administration input, taking into account the factors such as community, the nature of the learner, etc., which might modify the goals or influence their achievement; 2) Determination of classroom activities by the teacher and/or additional parties, taking previous factors into account; 3) Continual monitoring and evaluation of achievement of the goals set in step 1.

FIGURE 1

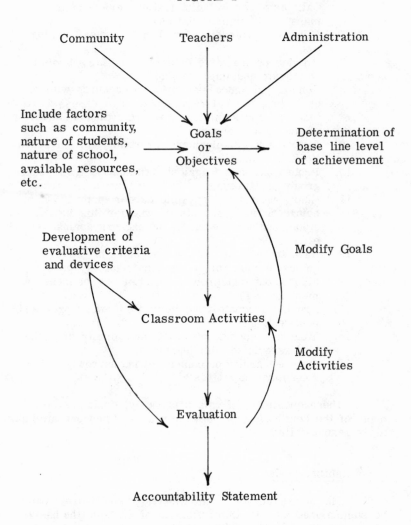

On the basis of data in step 3, other steps are implemented and /or modified and a continual cycle is established. It is important to note that the emphasis in this accountability model is on internal accountability and continual modification, rather than on a summative evaluation and a final accountability statement. It seems that by emphasizing the formative accountability, we may be able to avoid much of the conflict inherent in a final summative report, while retaining the best features of the process--namely, the delineation of goals and continuous monitoring of achievement. It might also be pointed out that this model bears a strong resemblance to the Tyler (9) rationale of curriculum construction, which has formed the basis of many generations of curricula.

The final consideration in examining a model is "can it be implemented?" Lopez (5) has developed an approach to implementation of accountability. Basically, Lopez suggests that everyone involved must get together and develop a charter of responsibility and accountability. In this charter the roles are spelled out, the nature of accountability is defined, and the measures are spelled out. Again, we must emphasize that during this process the safeguard questions (8) must also be asked and resolved.

It is clear from the discussion that no accountability process will yield final answers or data on which individual teachers can be promoted or demoted. However, if the emphasis is shifted from a final judgment of performance to an ongoing evaluation, with an emphasis on improved classroom conditions rather than on teacher (or school) ranking, and if the emphasis is on developing a working (if not perfect) charter of responsibility, then accountability may prove to be a viable concept for the improvement of urban education.

Notes

1. Barro, Stephen M. "An Approach to Developing Accountability Measures for the Public Schools," Phi Delta Kappan 52:4 (December 1970), 196-205.

2. "Report Shows Chicago Pupils Lag on National Tests," Chicago Sun-Times 26:125 (September 17, 1973), 3.

3. Dyer, Henry S., "Toward Objective Criteria of Professional Accountability in the Schools of New York City, "

Phi Delta Kappan 52:4 (December 1970), 206-211.

4. Lieberman, Myron W. , "An Overview of Accountability, "
    Phi Delta Kappan 52:4 (December 1970), 194-195.

5. Lopez, Felix M. , "Accountability in Education, " Phi
    Delta Kappan 52:4 (December 1970), 231-235.

6. McDonald, Frederick J. and Forehand, Garlie A. , "A
    Design for Accountability in Education, " New York
    University Education Quarterly 4:2 (Winter 1973), 7-16.

7. Ornstein, Allan C. and Talmage, Harriet, "A Dissenting
    View on Accountability, " Urban Education 8:3 (July
    1973), 133-152.

8. Ornstein, Allan C. and Talmage, Harriet, "The Rhetoric
    and the Realities of Accountability, " Today's Education
    62:6 (September-October 1973), 70-80.

9. Tyler, Ralph W. , Basic Principles of Curriculum and
    Instruction.   (Chicago, Illinois: University of Chicago
    Press, 1951).

14. A CLASSROOM MODEL FOR THE EDUCATION OF CULTURAL MINORITY PUPILS

Bert O. Richmond

"We may arbitrarily define culturally disadvantaged youth as those who are the products of a culture that has not provided them with the motivations, opportunities, experiences, and relationships that will enhance their chances for competing successfully with their fellow citizens in all phases of life. " (1)

The "culturally disadvantaged" child continues to be a challenge to education although considerable research and effort in innovative educational experiences provide insight into his limited progress in school. Some of the general findings are that the culturally disadvantaged child lives in a neighborhood of economically-deprived families who possess low social status in our society. The family unit is apt to be larger than the average and may contain relatives other than parents and siblings. The home is often marked by parental discord, in part due to the father's inability to obtain and maintain employment commensurate with his personal needs and the family's financial needs. Thus, divorce and desertion of the father are higher than average (9). There is also a higher rate of illegitimate births and migration of the family from one residence to another (1). Young children in these families are often left to care for themselves or are entrusted to older siblings or an adult relative in order for the mother to accept a position in unskilled labor that maintains her family at a poverty level. Often the family subsists in whole or in part on private charity and governmental welfare programs. Adult members of these family units are below average in educational level, and demonstrate a value system and

Bert O. Richmond, "A Classroom Model for the Education of Cultural Minority Pupils, " Education (February-March 1972), pp. 8-12. Reprinted by permission of the author and publisher.

style of language different from that of the middle class
American. The life style of economically deprived families
tends to place less emphasis on reading books and on intellectual discussions by the family than is found in culturally
advantaged homes. Due in large part to necessity, the economically deprived family concerns itself with the immediate
and practical goals of sufficient food, clothing, and shelter.
Books, cultural events, travel, and intellectual discourse are
luxuries that few can afford financially or have had the opportunity to learn to appreciate. Thus, their style of work,
recreations, and leisure activities tend to be action-oriented
rather than introspective (3).

From this environmental experience, the child entering an educational experience more characterized by middle
class values learns to see himself in an alien culture (6, 7).
He is different and his uniqueness seems to him to have less
value than that of the advantaged child. As a result of his
early life experiences, he finds upon entering school that labels of mental retardation, slow-learner and underachiever
are typical for one of his background (11). In addition, his
resorting to the use of physical strength or slang language to
solve problems; his poverty of verbal fluency and failure to
achieve a desired social status in school earn him labels
such as emotionally-disturbed, discipline problem, or juvenile
delinquent. Sensing the rejection of his style of life by both
peers and adults and realizing that he does not achieve the
goals espoused in the educational setting he develops a compensatory behavior. He may become more truant and more
rebellious in order to fight back against the people and the
system that he views responsible for his failure (4).

He is likely to be a member of a minority group such
as Negro, Indian, Mexican-American or Appalachian (1) and
may seek an even closer affiliation with other members of his
own group. Another typical form of compensatory behavior
is to withdraw in the face of forces which he feels unable to
resist and thus he reinforces feelings of his personal inade-
quacy and rejection (2). The culturally deprived child, re-
gardless of his method of coping with a strange and alien
culture, usually has a low self-concept (8) and is constricted
in interpersonal relationships and in verbal communications
(10). Therefore, an educational experience that is to be
meaningful for this child must take into account his feelings
and his limited experiences. It is necessary not only to compensate for cultural limitations but to enhance his feelings
of self-worth through greater self-understanding. Greater

acceptance by his teachers and peers can free him to develop intellectual capacities and to achieve more complete self-expression.

In planning a program to enhance the educational experiences of children from cultural minority groups it is helpful to understand their environmental background but also necessary to remember that each child is unique. Not every disadvantaged child will reveal the same deficits or strengths; therefore, a meaningful educational program must strive to be responsive to each child's abilities, interests, and needs.

In the traditional classroom, a premium is placed on individual initiative. A concept is introduced or an assignment given and each child in the class is expected to solve the problem on his own. Getting help from other students or adults in this process of problem-solving may be interpreted as "cheating" and result in an assessment of failure on the child's part. Yet in the adult world, decision making is rarely, if ever, an individual effort. Scientists and researchers cooperate and rely on the findings of previous experimenters in extending interpretations of evidence in their own fields. Staff conferences in business and education are an accepted technique of policy-making. Few legislators at any level of government want to propose a solution to a problem unless a majority of their constituency support the solution.

Such cooperation in problem-solving appears to be necessary in a democratic society. It not only provides a maximum amount of support to implement a decision but it encourages the attainment of goals for the common good rather than those defined more by forces of individual expediency.

Cooperation in solving educational problems appears to offer some distinct advantages to the disadvantaged child. It places less strain on an already lowered self-concept to know that the task is shared by other students who have achieved greater success with this kind of task. It lowers the anxiety associated with failure to know that the responsibility for success is jointly shared. The interaction among peers in a cooperative effort provides greater opportunity to understand and accept the limitations and strengths which each brings to the total effort. We must understand that maximum educational intervention can occur only if it affects the cultural minority group member in his social realm.

The model proposed for this cooperative educational
effort is the Peer Group Learning Unit. In the elementary
classroom consisting of 25-30 pupils, four such units would
be formed. Each unit would have approximately equal numbers of pupils, equated for sex, racial characteristics, and
degree of cultural advantage in order that each learning unit
is representative of the total school and community. All
children in a given grade would be assigned randomly to
classrooms serving their residential area. Then children
in each classroom would be assigned to the Peer Group
Learning Units within each classroom to reflect the hetero-
geneous nature of the community. Although these units should
remain stable throughout the school year, adjustments could be
made to accommodate individual pupil needs, a changing school
population, or other factors that necessitate such change. The
number of pupils in each Peer Group Learning Unit is arbi-
trary. It would fluctuate some depending upon the number of
pupils in a classroom, the skill of pupils and teacher in group
problem solving, as well as the physical arrangement of the
classroom. A minimum number in each unit would ordinarily
be 5 or 6 in order to stratify properly for such variables as
sex, ability, and cultural differences. The physical arrangement of the classroom must allow for and encourage separate
small groups participation. In the experience of the author,
the most satisfactory arrangement in a self-contained classroom is to have four tables with chairs for these groups.
Each group is spaced as far as possible from other groups
to allow for active and sometimes noisy participation by each
group member.

It is not necessary to depart from the usual curriculum of the elementary school, with two important exceptions.
This means that basically the same subject matter could be
presented and that each child taking advantage of special
musical education, speech therapy, 4-H clubs and the like
would be free to leave his unit at the appropriate time.
There would be two enriching experiences added to the curriculum. One of these would have the objective of self-understanding and the other self-expression.

In the self-understanding experience, children would
discuss and engage in activities designed to help them understand and accept themselves and thereby to develop an understanding and acceptance of others. For example, the teacher
may assist the group in learning about differences among people but will help them to focus on the similarities of needs,
aspirations, strengths, and weaknesses of the individual re-

gardless of his major referent cultural group. Examples of classroom exercises designed to elicit this kind of understanding are:

1. What Kind of Person Are You?
2. What Behavior Do We Admire in People?
3. What Are Your Interests?
4. What Are Your Abilities?
5. In What Way Is Each Person in this Classroom Unique?
6. What Kind of Person Would You Like to Be?
7. What Kind of Behavior Causes Pupils to have Conflict with Peers? Parents? Teachers?
8. Describe the Kind of Person You Like Best. Least.

These examples are only a few of the topics that can be approached directly or indirectly to enable pupils to think and discuss characteristics of self as well as interpersonal relationships. A variety of techniques can be used to facilitate this kind of learning such as role-playing, written exercises, group discussion, art and music media. A conflict within the classroom or on the playground provides an excellent opportunity for pupils to learn to use communication to resolve differences and at the same time gain a deeper insight into the causes for human behavior. The self-understanding experience should be provided for a total of thirty minutes during each day of school. It may be presented as a structured experience each day or used spontaneously as relations within the classroom, school, or community suggest its utility. The teacher must be skillful in implementing this experience to prevent pupils from perceiving it as an adult criticism of children's behavior and values or as an opportunity to attack defenseless members of the group. Objectivity in understanding and accepting different points of view is critical to the success of the group leader in this experience. The teacher must also be skilled in understanding when and how to support individuals in the classroom.

In the self-expression experience each Peer Group Learning Unit has the responsibility for defining and pursuing a group-determined learning problem. For example, one unit may decide that it wishes to learn more about lunar probes and must thereby decide whether to consult newspapers, encyclopedias, or other sources for this information. Another unit may consider it important to demonstrate to the classroom some special skills or interests of each member of

its group.   At the end of the week, each unit might report
orally the results of its efforts in group-determined learning
to the total classroom.   Leadership in delineating the problem
to explore, solution of the problem, and the report of findings
to the total class should rotate among members of the unit
and involve each member.   This sharing of responsibility is
necessary to elicit maximum self-expression by each pupil.
This experience should also be given at least thirty minutes
each day with additional time for field-trip explorations or
other group effort on the problem after the regular classroom
assignments are completed.   When handled skillfully by the
teacher, both of these special addenda blend with and comple-
ment the usual curriculum.

        The role of the teacher differs somewhat in this kind
of classroom.   She remains responsible for presenting the
basic concept, information, or skill necessary to the child's
growth in each subject area.   She may present an educational
objective to the entire class, followed by a reading practice
or other assignment to enable them to demonstrate that they
understand the concept or information or have acquired the
skill required.   It then becomes the responsibility of the
Peer Group Learning Unit to demonstrate a group mastery
of the assignment.   Each pupil is given the responsibility to
contribute to the total group accomplishment.   The teacher is
free to move from unit to unit to encourage the involvement
of all members in problem-solving.   At the same time, she
can assess the nature of each pupil's contribution to problem-
solving and assist in strengthening his deficiencies.   The
teacher can foster a spirit of group solution to problems and
help to prevent group rejection toward one member or with-
drawal from participation by any group member.   In addition,
the teacher serves as a resource person to each unit to further explain a concept and to stimulate pupil persistence
toward meaningful problem-solving.   Initially, it is often
necessary for the teacher to encourage pupils to rely more
on themselves than on her.   The pupils soon learn to trust
their own experiences and view the teacher as facilitator
rather than director of their efforts.

        This model was used in classrooms containing cul-
tural minority pupils both in the Southeast and in a large
midwestern urban area.   There were some problems encountered in its implementation.   A few teachers complained that
pupils were too noisy and did not learn what they were sup-
posed to.   There were some embarrassing moments when a
child openly condemned his family's interaction or began to

ridicule an unpopular classmate. There were also infrequent but probing queries from the building principal concerning the nature of the classroom experiences.

The vast majority of the experiences reported in these classrooms were favorable. Even the embarrassing incidents contributed to the insights gained by teachers and pupils. Noise seems to be a necessary by-product of 30 people communicating in one room but the children began to understand that curtailment of excess noise made it easier for them to work as a group. The building principals were more concerned about understanding than preventing changes in classroom procedure.

The pupils were generally unanimous in preferring the freedom of this kind of classroom. Pupils who were previously frightened or hostile at the suggestion of a quiet, tension-packed two minute report to the class learned that their ideas were worthwhile and respected by the entire group. "Talking things over" became a meaningful experience for most of them. The shy ones learned quickly that their efforts to explain a concept would be supported by other members of the group. Their major complaints were about the member of a group who did not contribute and frequently this social pressure resulted in greater involvement from the formerly involved. The most provocative appraisal of this model came from a teacher who stated that it allowed her to help rather than force children to learn.

There are some reported research evidences (5, 12) that all of us may know more than any one of us. Certainly there is experience from a variety of human endeavors to warrant education's venture into the substitution of cooperation for competition as the major incentive for the child's growth.

Notes

1. Amos, W. E. "The nature of disadvantaged youth." Counseling the Disadvantaged Youth, W. E. Amos and J. D. Grambs, Eds. Englewood Cliffs, N.J.: Prentice-Hall, 1968.

2. Bernstein, B. "Social Class, Speech Systems, and Psycho-Therapy" F. Riessman, J. Cohen and A. Pearl. Mental Health of the Poor, New York: The Free Press of Glencoe, Inc., 1964.

3. Deutsch, M. et al. "Some Considerations as to the
    Contributions of Social, Personality, and Racial Factors
    to School Retardation in Minority Group Children."
    Paper read at American Psychological Association,
    Chicago, September, 1956.

4. Gordon, J. E. "Counseling the Disadvantaged Boy."
    Counseling the Disadvantaged Youth. W. E. Amos
    & J. D. Grambs, Eds. Englewood Cliffs, N.J.;
    Prentice-Hall, 1968.

5. Maier, N. R. F. Problem Solving and Creativity.
    Belmont, Calif.: Brooks, Cole, 1970.

6. Margolin, J. "The Mental Health of the Disadvantaged"
    Counseling the Disadvantaged Youth. Englewood
    Cliffs, N.J.: Prentice-Hall, 1968.

7. Merton, R. K. Social Theory & Social Structure, rev.
    ed. New York: The Free Press of Glencoe, Inc.,
    1957.

8. Orem, R. C. "Language and the Culturally Disadvan-
    taged" Counseling the Disadvantaged Youth. Engle-
    wood Cliffs, N.J.: Prentice-Hall, 1968.

9. Orshansky, M. "Counting the Poor: another look at
    the poverty profile." Poverty In America. J. L.
    Kornbluh and A. Haber, eds. Ann Arbor: Univer-
    sity of Michigan Press, 1965.

10. Pasamanick, B. & Knoblock, H. "Early Language
    Behavior in Negro Children and the Testing of
    Intelligence." Journal of Abnormal and Social Psy-
    chology, 50 (1955), 401-402.

11. Riessman, Frank, "The Culturally Deprived Child: A
    New View" Programs for the Educationally Disad-
    vantaged. U.S. Dept. of Health, Education & Welfare.
    Washington, D.C.: Government Printing Office,
    1968, p. 8.

12. Wechsler, D. Concept of Collective Intelligence.
    American Psychologist, 26:10 (1971), 904-907.

15. A REALISTIC VIEW OF HOMEWORK
FOR THE GHETTO CHILD

R. Baird Shuman and Henry L. Sublett, Jr.

Through the years most people have blandly considered that homework is part of the student's lot and that it is
essentially a good and wholesome activity which will teach
students to organize their free time and to develop the sort
of discipline which will make success in life surer for them.
There are indications that parents approve of homework because they "feel that more homework improves their children's
chances for college" and that "heavy homework assignments
are the best indication that their children are receiving 'quality education."[1] Of approximately 400 articles on homework
which have been written between 1928 and 1970,[2] an over-
whelming majority are in favor of homework assignments.
The National Education Association's Research Division,
gathering its facts from a broad assortment of elementary
school teachers, found that 83.5 per cent of those questioned
were generally in favor of homework,[3] although another study,
conducted over a narrower range, lists 48 per cent of the
elementary school teachers responding as feeling that students
would have gained more from a homework assignment had it
been done in class as part of the regular class work.[4]

But, as everyone knows, statistics can be used to
prove nearly anything and within the large corpus of professional writing on the subject of homework, all sorts of con-
tradictory facts, near-facts, and opinions can be found. Some
arguments against homework are as persuasive as the many
in favor of it. One can reasonably surmise, however, that
for a number of reasons--most notable among them the great
knowledge explosion that is evident throughout the civilized

R. Baird Shuman and Henry L. Sublett, Jr., "A Realistic
View of Homework for the GHETTO CHILD," The Clearing
House (November 1970), pp. 140-145. Reprinted by permis-
sion of the authors and publisher.

world today[5]--homework assignments will continue to be a
common phenomenon in most of the schools in this nation.

As one reads numerous statements regarding homework, one is struck by a number of items on which one can
base generalizations:

    (1) Most writers still think in terms of a read-write-
        recite sort of homework situation. Homework is
        generally still viewed as a sedentary occupation.

    (2) Homework is essentially viewed as an activity for
        the middle- and upper-class student, since most
        writers contend that the student must have a clean,
        well-lighted, well-ventilated, quiet place in which
        to work. Few disadvantaged children are able to
        find such ideal surroundings in which to work;
        hence, in the typical situation, they are immediate-
        ly handicapped.

    (3) Many writers still think of homework assignments
        as day-to-day rather than as long term, project-
        centered assignments.

    (4) Many writers still begin with the spurious and un-
        fortunate assumption that homework assignments
        must be "blanket" rather than individualized as-
        signments.

In schools throughout America's far-flung and all too
numerous ghettos, many teachers have just given up in their
attempts to have their students do any work outside of school.
Most teachers in such situations know from hearsay if not
from personal experience and observation that their students
come from crowded, run-down apartments, some of which
have not even the most rudimentary sanitary facilities. They
know that some of their students not only lack a quiet, well-
lighted place in which to study, but also share a broken-
down bed in a rat infested room with two or three siblings
every night of their lives. They know that many of their
students, even in the senior high school years, have not
achieved basic literacy and probably never will. They know
that two-room apartments in the hard-core slum areas often
provide shelter for six or eight or even ten people. They
know, and they bleed inside from the knowledge, and they die
a little bit every day, and they eventually flee the ghettos in
huge numbers because this is not what they went into teaching
for.

But what of the ghetto kid? He cannot flee in any
real sense except to another ghetto. He has nowhere to turn.
If a boy, he becomes a hustler and/or a pusher. If a girl,
she gets pregnant in desperation so that she can have her own
welfare check, her own dark room or two, and the cycle
starts all over again. The seeds of America's destruction
as a world power are germinating at an alarming rate in a
ghetto situation which is growing like the cells in an advanced case of melanoma. And in most cases, teachers
and school administrators, people of conscience who find
themselves utterly stymied, last for the short while that it
takes them to reach the limits of human endurance, and then,
often for the sake of self-preservation, they turn from that
which is too horrible for them to face any longer.

But the youngsters caught in the trap of the ghetto
cannot run screaming--and many of them cannot survive as,
for example, twelve-year-old Walter Vandermeer, a child
of the ghetto, who died last December from an overdose of
heroin. [6] One of the most haunting lines in Julius Horwitz's
exceptionally perceptive book about the ghetto, The Diary of
A. N. , [7] comes under the protagonist's entry for April 22
(p. 27): "If I don't write in my diary every day it is because some days are too terrible to write about. "

The Diary of A. N. is a work of fiction; but it is so
strongly based upon Horwitz's background in social work in
the New York City ghettos that it is essentially a documentary
in a fictional frame. In the book, the fifteen-year-old black
protagonist bares her heart to the reading public, a public
which should include every school teacher in the nation--even
those teaching in the most affluent reaches of suburbia.

School means a great deal to A. N. It is the only
hope in her life, the only thing upon which she can depend.
Teachers in the ghetto come and go, often driven away within a few days by the desperate situations which they find
there. But one teacher, Miss A. , lasts through the two
years which the Diary covers, and she becomes the most
significant influence in A. N. 's life. This is so because
Miss A. has not given up on her students, and they know it.
When Miss A. is absent, A. N. writes, "I miss Miss A.
She tries to get us to do some work in class" (p. 23). Miss
A. is not like the other teachers who "seem to think they
are wasting their knowledge on us" (pp. 93-94). Rather
"Miss A. is a real English teacher. She gives me lists of
books to read and asks me questions about the books to make

sure that I know what I read. This is just between us, after
class" (p. 43).

Students of whom little is expected will produce little.
Herein is one of the major problems in ghetto education. But
it is likely that no contemporary educational problem presents
the challenge that ghetto education presents today. Finding a
means to reach ghetto children should be to the educator what
finding a cure for cancer is to the physician. And the starting point in finding a solution to this problem comes with
analyzing what some of the major elements of the problem
are. The most salient elements can be listed rather simply:

(1) Grinding poverty.
(2) Lack of hope for the future.
(3) Nowhere to turn.
(4) Breakdown of the family structure.
(5) Alienation from the mainstream of society.
(6) Deterioration of self-respect.
(7) Drug addiction.
(8) The feeling of being dealt with unjustly.

Actually, the school can meet or help to meet many
of these problems, but it absolutely cannot do so within the
sort of academic context in which "most of the teachers'
energy goes into control."[8] An emphasis on control is a
clear indication of an outmoded and meaningless curriculum.
Everyone wants to learn something. The major problem in
ghetto schools today is that students do not generally wish to
learn what the school feels it must teach them.

How can some of the above problems be met by the
school? Certainly the first two can at least be broached if
the school provides work opportunity for students which will
make it possible for them to receive a salary while receiving
credit for attending school. Distributive education programs
have made great contributions in some areas, and the contributions have been to the business community as well as to the
students involved.

It is obvious that the third element listed, "Nowhere
to turn," can be attacked in part just by a teacher's willing-
ness to listen and discuss. However, a much broader approach than this may be taken. To begin with, students must
have some voice in deciding upon curriculum which is meaningful to them. School provides someplace to turn, but it
cannot do so if the curriculum is irrelevant to the students

involved.   In ghetto areas, it is significant that school attendance is at its highest on bitterly cold days, days when snow
softens even the harsh, begrimed outlines of the ghetto.   On
such days, schools in suburbia might be closed; or, if open,
attendance is very low.   But to the ghetto dweller, the hostili-
ty of nature is very real because he does not have the where-
withal to fight it.   He cannot afford to keep his dwelling warm
and dry and cozy.   Ghetto kids keep warm in school.

Schoolmen should take this fact as a clue which they
might use in making the school more serviceable to youngsters.   If students need a quiet, well-lighted, well-ventilated
place in which to study, why should the school not stay open
until nine o'clock at least two evenings a week so that students
might come to study under supervision?   To keep one large
classroom open, supervised by two or three teachers given
supplementary salary for their supervision, would be to provide a place in which homework might be done.   It would also
do a great deal to make the school more a part of the ghetto
child's life.

It would be naive to assume that keeping the school
open would not cause problems.   In New York City for instance, in which there are conservatively estimated to be
over 25, 000 teen-aged heroin addicts, [9] heroin would be shot
and pills popped in the school were it to stay open in the evening.   But heroin is shot and pills are popped in schools
during the day and on the roofs of tenement buildings at
night, so this is really not a convincing argument against
keeping the schools open.   The question of cost must undoubtedly be raised.   In terms of conventional bookkeeping,
such a program would cost the school district money; but in
terms of reduced crime in the streets, society would be the
beneficiary, and society provides the monies on which schools
operate.

One progressive school district, realizing just how
difficult it is for deprived youngsters to do anything academic
outside the school setting, has provided places and tutors to
youngsters who have no adequate place to study.   Montgomery
County, Maryland has established 14 study groups serving 850
students who might otherwise have no facilities for home
study.   The Montgomery County program is staffed by three
paid supervisors and 500 volunteers. [10] Through it, youngsters
who once had nowhere to turn now know where to turn, and
having turned, they will become more productive human beings.

The school cannot do very much about the breakdown of
the family structure in ghetto areas, but it can do all in its
power not to enlarge the fissures which already exist. For
example, a ghetto child should not be asked, as A. N. was,
to write "a report about my father" (p. 121). This is an embarrassing topic for many ghetto kids. Nor should the school
do anything to cause the child to think that the level of language to which he is daily exposed in his natural environment
is substandard or incorrect. If the study of grammar serves
any purpose in ghetto schools, it is that of demonstrating to
students that there are many ways of speaking and that each
way is appropriate to its own situation.

The child who is alienated from his society usually
sees the school and its personnel as fundamental parts of the
society from which he is alienated. Until the school demonstrates to him that it can deal with his needs, he will remain
alienated; it is as simple as that. Therefore, in ghetto situations particularly, human considerations must precede and
take priority over substantive, narrowly academic considerations. For this reason, Cunningham's suggestion of permitting the principals and faculties of ghetto schools to have
greater autonomy[11] makes very good sense.

No one who fails constantly can achieve self-respect.
Therefore, built into any educational system and into every
homework assignment must be provisions and opportunities
for students to experience a degree of success. This is why
narrowly conceived curricular considerations are archaic in
an educational system aimed at providing free, public education for the masses. If a student works within a situation
in which he begins to experience success, his achievement
will increase, and his whole self-image will be greatly en-
hanced. Rather than viewing education as a barrier, he will
come to view it, quite reasonably, as the bridge between him
and the sort of life which he most desires.

The drug problem is so great and its implications so
far-reaching that the schools, particularly those in ghetto
areas, must wage a forceful and realistic attack upon it.
This probably means that every ghetto school must have a
cadre of expert medical personnel available to it. Also, the
drug problem should be discussed openly and freely in class
and students should be encouraged to seek help without fear
that punitive measures will be taken against them either by
legal agencies or by other students in the school who perhaps
are encouraging their addiction. Only in a climate of free

communication can this problem be tackled with even a
modicum of success.

Finally, students resent nothing more than unjust treatment. They can bear disappointment, they can survive many
difficulties; but if the cards seem to be stacked against them,
if they are the victims of bigotry and prejudgment from those
who represent the dominant society, they will react violently
and will have no respect for the law. Teachers must be very
sure that they act deliberately and reasonably in dealing with
students, for they, by so doing, can become the models after
which students will create their own behavioral patterns.

The question of homework for the ghetto student is a
most important one. The assigning of homework gives the
student the feeling that something is expected of him. Assignments should be individualized as much as possible and should
be related to the life which the student knows and must come
to understand better. A conventional assignment of reading a
chapter and answering questions on it or of doing ten mathematics problems is an unfair assignment for a youngster who
does not have an adequate place to work. If the school cannot
be open to him in the late afternoon and evening, probably his
homework assignments should be centered around something
that he can do in his neighborhood or in the neighborhood library.   In the latter case, it would be well for the teacher to
become acquainted with the staff of the public library serving
the area which the school serves. In the former case, the
teacher must do some homework as well as the student: he
must come to know the neighborhood, its people, its buildings,
its facilities.   Then he must work with all of his creative
energy to suggest homework assignments which can capitalize
on what the student has available to him.   As Marcia Drake,
a teacher dealing with impoverished youngsters in Seaside,
California, states, "It's too easy to blame poverty for the
cultural gulf that separates school and students--it lets the
school off the hook.   Instead, we have to take the initiative
in building bridges; we can't wait for the kids to improve
their own environment."[12]

The teacher working with the ghetto child must be
aware of his frustrations and limitations.   But he must also
be aware that the student's self-respect will develop only if
he is called upon to produce both in school and on his own
through out-of-school assignments. These assignments must
make sense to the students and they must be dealt with by
the teacher as important adjuncts to learning. Nothing which

is of vital concern to any child can be viewed as lying outside
the curriculum. Teachers need to realize that the ghetto
child represents a staggering paradox in that he is at once
extremely sophisticated in many ways and yet so parochial
in others; while he may have experienced parenthood on the
one hand, he might never have been more than a mile away
from his own street, so that the center of his own city may
be completely unknown to him.

For the ghetto student, the in-school experience is
perhaps less vital than directed experience out-of-school, for
it is in the area beyond the walls of the school in which he
has had to develop and cultivate his independence to survive.
The teacher who realizes this, and who provides for the student's needs by giving him extramural assignments through
which he can increase his understanding of himself and his
environment, has made a significant stride toward bringing
desperately troubled youngsters to the brink of self-realiza-
tion.

Notes

1. George W. Bond and George J. Smith, "Establishing a
    Homework Program," The Elementary School Journal,
    LXVI (1965), p. 139.

2. Robert L. Kerzic, "The Value of Homework," The
    Clearing House, XLI (1966), pp. 140-142. Kerzic
    states that The Education Index from 1928-1965 lists
    in excess of 350 articles dealing with ... homework."

3. National Educational Association, Research Division,
    "Elementary School Homework," NEA Journal, LI
    (1961), p. 53.

4. John A. Mengel, John Holcroft, and Richard D. Zahn,
    "Attitudes toward Homework," The Elementary School
    Journal, LXVII (1966), p. 43.

5. For a discussion of this see the comment of James
    Moon quoted by Marilyn H. Cutter in "How Much
    Homework Is Enough?" Nation's Schools, LXXVII
    (1966), p. 65.

6. Time, XCV (March 16, 1970), p. 16.

7. New York: Coward-McCann, Inc., 1970.

8. Luvern L. Cunningham. "Hey, Man, You Our Princi-
    pal?" Education Digest, XXXV (February, 1970),
    p. 7.

9. "Kids and Heroin: The Adolescent Epidemic," Time,
    op. cit., p. 16.

10. M. Buskin. "Problem: How to Provide Adequate
    Home Study Facilities and Opportunities for Disad-
    vantaged Negro Students," School Management, XI
    (1967), pp. 66-67.

11. Cunningham, op. cit., p. 8.

12. Quoted in James Solberg. "I Want Them to Know That
    We Care," School Management, XII (1968), p. 41.

16. IS STUDENT TEACHING BANKRUPT?

Philip D. Vairo and William Perel

Within academic circles, both the supporters and the
critics of the faculties of our colleges of education assume
that their chief function is to teach prospective teachers how
to teach. Actually, in many colleges of education we have
found that this function is considered the least important by
those members of the faculty supposedly charged with preparing teachers. Most professors of education are likely to be
concerned with their research, with course work in philosophy
or history of education, or with the preparation of persons for
school administration. Many view a promotion as a chance to
escape from involvement with teacher training. Nowhere is
this attitude more evident than in the practices and procedures
for student teaching.

Unfortunately, the most important aspect of teacher
training, the student teaching internship, has taken on an unpleasant connotation. The colleges and universities, the public schools, and the profession as a whole have given this
matter very little, if any, serious consideration. Little or
no effort has been made to develop an internship for the prospective teacher that represents a well-planned program. On
the whole, attempts have been feeble and unworthy of the profession. There is little comparison, for example, between
the professional experience required of a medical intern and
that required of the student teacher. At best, student teaching is a superficial exposure. The short duration of the internship plus inadequate supervision and first-hand experience does
little to prepare students for classroom leadership. For these
and other reasons, we say that student teaching is bankrupt
and needs a total re-evaluation.

Philip D. Vairo and William Perel, "Is Student Teaching
Bankrupt?" The Clearing House (April 1968), pp. 451-455.
Reprinted by permission of the authors and publisher.

Some of our schools have proceeded on the naive assumption that students sent to them by the colleges and universities for student teaching already know how to teach or will learn on the job by a process of trial and error. Student teaching programs are often haphazard affairs with a minimum amount of direction and coordination. Although there is a need to reduce the faculty-student teacher ratio considerably, many colleges have a student-teacher ratio of at least 20 to 1 during student teaching.

The Cooperating Teacher

During his internship the student teacher is over-whelmed with many chores which divert his attention from real teaching and which complicate and frustrate the objectives of the experience. The cooperating teacher also has many demands placed upon him. He is expected to be a chaperon, a public relations man, a personal friend, and an excellent teacher. There is urgent need for clarification of the role of the cooperating teacher. Should he not be considered a member of the college faculty? His duties are certainly vital to the teacher education program. Why not recognize the cooperating teacher as a professional colleague in fact as well as in spirit?

It must be said that the cooperating teacher must be a person of sufficient competence to be respected by those student teachers whom he is to supervise. Certainly, as a minimum qualification, we should demand that a cooperating teacher hold a master's degree in the teaching field and have at least three years of teaching experience. Further, he ought to have received some relatively recent training through workshops, institutes, or short courses. Such programs supported by the National Science Foundation or by the Office of Education are now fairly common, and there is no reason why teachers with such experiences would not be available in most areas. Certainly, the supervising teacher ought to have a sufficiency of both subject matter knowledge and teaching experience to enable him to make constructive suggestions to the young novice. Unfortunately, it sometimes happens that the cooperating teacher is less competent than are some of the student teachers he is expected to supervise. In such cases the resentment of the student teacher being supervised is readily understandable.

Further, to give a teacher the title "cooperating

teacher" and then give him no reduction in his own teaching
load or additional compensation is to pretend that the student
teacher does not need special help which is time-consuming
for the cooperating teacher. In such cases, the cooperating
teacher is only a device by which the college administration
and the public schools can relieve themselves of some of the
details of student teacher supervision. In no real sense can
a cooperating teacher give attention to the supervision of a
student teacher within his classroom, while he is himself
teaching a full load of courses! Remuneration without a
course load reduction is not the answer either, as there are
only so many hours in each day.

          The failure to recognize the efforts of the cooperating
teacher often leads him to adopt a cynical attitude, and simply
use his student teachers to divest himself of some of his work
load. Why should we expect a teacher who has not received
special training in supervision, and who is not regarded by
either his superiors or by the college authorities as one who
is making an important contribution to teacher education, to
regard his role as sufficiently important to give it his fullest
attention?

Supervising the Student Teacher

          Another stumbling block has been that mutual observa-
tion among student teachers and experienced teachers has run
head-on into our tradition of respecting the so-called privacy
of the teacher in his classroom. Older teachers and depart-
mental chairmen should be encouraged to visit the classes
taught by the student teacher, and the student teacher should
be encouraged to visit their classes. We have found this
practice to be the exception rather than the rule.

          One of the basic principles of supervision is that it assist
a teacher in utilizing to the maximum his abilities and resources. There is little doubt that every teacher possesses
strengths and capabilities of which he may not even be aware
or which are not integrated fully into the teaching situation.
With professional guidance and direction the student teacher
can identify and assess his strengths and resources. Helping
the young teacher to develop a sense of security and a realistic
self-appraisal are essential attributes of the cooperating teacher
and college supervisor. However, as long as the student
teacher is assigned a grade for the experience, a strange
relationship exists between supervisor and student. Why must

a grade be assigned? Would not pass or fail suffice? Physicians are required to complete an internship as a condition for licensing, but they are not assigned grades.

The cooperating teacher and college supervisor must have the capacity for professional interpretation to the teacher. Student teachers may not be psychologically ready to explore their own resources, and the cooperating teacher and college supervisor will both need to relate in a positive, constructive fashion if they are to help the student teacher's functioning. Needless to say, it is not their function to provide wholesale recipes for classroom situations and techniques of teaching. Present supervisory practices such as the convenient "check list" in many instances are as archaic as would be the horse and buggy on Madison Avenue.

If the "Big Brother" attitude conveyed by Carbone[1] exists in most supervisory situations, which we believe may well be the case in some schools, there is little doubt that supervision is not providing the necessary ingredients to assist either the classroom teacher or the student teacher. Although perhaps exaggerating the point, Carbone suggests that teachers tend to think that the supervisor is always trying to check up on them--even going so far as to tune in their classes on the intercom system. This negative attitude towards supervision is often conveyed to the student teacher by the experienced teachers. In a recent popular novel set in a New York high school, the teachers referred to the possibility of visits by their department chairmen with the phrase "the ghost walks." Such attitudes seem to be fairly common in real life, as well. But only with proper supervision and understanding may a student teacher develop into an adequate teacher, and a mediocre teacher develop into an outstanding classroom performer. We believe that the present practices do not lend themselves to a wholesome professional experience.

Supervision should not be restricted to visits on specific pre-arranged dates. An open visit, however, is much to be preferred over electronic eavesdropping.

During the student teaching experience, while the tyro is subject to the supervision of a cooperating teacher, much improvement ought to be possible. But most cooperating teachers have had no special training in supervision, not even so much as one course. Why should not some course work in supervision be part of the master's program for a teacher, who,

having earned a master's degree, should be in a position to
offer leadership in teaching? If the cooperating teacher has
only a bachelor's degree and only two or three years of
teaching experience, it is very common to find that the student teacher, having more recent training and perhaps at a
superior university or college, knows a great deal more about
his subject than does the cooperating teacher. If then, the
cooperating teacher knows neither more about the subject nor
more about the teaching or anything about supervision, it is
not surprising that he is not respected by the student teacher
who has been put in his charge. Under such circumstances,
the student teacher will find it difficult to accept such advice
and criticism as he is given. Even worse, the cooperating
teacher may be so insecure himself that he will not be able
to offer any advice or criticism.

Evaluating the Student Teacher

        Student evaluation should also be very much a part of
the student teaching experience. How can it be ignored? Although it is conceded that many students lack sound judgment, this limitation does not offset the fact that student responses can be helpful in many ways. The student teacher
and cooperating teacher can get some ideas about the attitudes
and reactions of the students. We seldom consult the students
who, after all, are the very reason we are attempting to improve instruction. Evaluation often comes from some administrative source. The students, even those in the early grades,
can offer valuable suggestions. Student opinion on the quality
of instruction is valuable only if properly interpreted, however. But in any program of student ratings, care must be
taken to avoid giving the students the impression that a student teacher obtains his grade at their pleasure. Surely students can be shown that their opinions are valued and respected, without turning the school over to student control.

        If the role of the cooperating teacher in the student
teaching experience is less than satisfactory, and if the students being taught are given no role at all, what of the role
of the university professor who is assigned to observe student
teachers? Many of these professors consider the function of
observing student teachers as not worthy of their professional
time. Particularly, as a professor rises in rank and seniority and becomes more and more involved with graduate programs, with all of the prestige and fringe benefits usually
associated with such involvement, he tends to lose interest

and concern in actively participating in this primary function
of his discipline, preparing teachers. Also, he finds that
his other activities leave him little time for such interest and
concern. Professors of education need to return to the public
school classroom every few years. There is no substitute
for first-hand, practical experience. Many professors of
education have been so long absent from the classroom themselves, that their training and experience have little relevance to the present-day teaching situation.

The college supervisor's purpose should be to assist
the student teacher in improving his teaching, rather than
simply to rate the teacher for the purpose of assigning a
grade. Care should be taken not to interrupt or embarrass
the student teacher in any way. Frequent, informal, short
visits are to be preferred to a few very long visits. Usually, more information may be obtained by weekly visits than
by even all-day visits at less frequent intervals.

After each classroom visit, the college supervisor and
cooperating teacher should confer with the student teacher in
private, and should discuss strengths as well as areas which
need improvement. Certainly, the college supervisor and cooperating teacher should both keep in mind the training and
experience of each student teacher, so that they can establish
realistic goals for him. If student teachers understand that
the information gained by visits to their classrooms will be
used to assign a grade and that they will not be evaluated by
gossip and hearsay, student teachers are more likely to wel-
come visits to their classrooms. Most of all, conferences
between the college supervisor and the cooperating teacher
should not be held in the teachers' lounge or in the department office, where other faculty are likely to be unwelcome
observers.

Both college supervisors and cooperating teachers
should encourage student teachers to prepare organized lesson
plans, rather than attempting to present their material in an
"off the cuff" fashion. All suggestions should be as clear and
concrete as possible, with the student teacher given an opportunity to present his ideas and opinions. Above all, the college supervisor should not get so lost in other college or university matters that he forgets that his first duty is to the
professional development of the student teachers.

Improving the Student Teaching Program

Let us attract the most qualified of our teacher education faculty to serve as college supervisors and not rely upon graduate assistants and young, inexperienced faculty for this important work. Also, colleges and universities should select with care the cooperating teachers. Often the cooperating teacher is selected by a school principal, without prior consultation with the college supervisor. And in some cases the cooperating teacher is required to accept the student teacher. For much too long, we have set our professional sights too low. The time has arrived for us to broaden them and develop a student teaching program of the first order.

We believe that the present status of the student teaching experience is so seriously deficient as to warrant the word "bankrupt." Unless considerable improvement can be made in the existing pattern, the time will come when we must consider changing the pattern altogether. Already, some criticism has been leveled at the present method of giving prospective teachers their practical experience. Typically, a student finds that the first half of his last semester in college is crowded with courses which have been especially devised to fit into half a semester, rather than those courses which would be the culmination of his advanced training. This procedure is established so that his student teaching experience may be crowded into the last eight weeks of his last semester. Perhaps the solution to the problem is to abandon student teaching as part of the undergraduate training of a prospective teacher. Perhaps the schools themselves must take a larger role in the training of teachers and provide something more like the one year internship now required of physicians. If the teaching profession is ever to be accorded the respect now given to the other professions, perhaps it will come when teachers are required to complete a full year of practical experience beyond their education.

We do not advocate so drastic a step as the abolition of the student teaching program, as it is now known. Before any thought should be given to abandoning the procedures now in use, a great deal of thought and study and effort should go into an attempt to make the present procedures work. What we advocate for the present is recognition that student teaching in its present form is bankrupt and that study, thought, and experimentation are vitally needed to remedy the most important gap in the entire teacher training program. We believe that student teaching can be made to work in the present

framework. But unless those in authority recognize that it
has not been working satisfactorily in the past, we shall either continue to produce unsatisfactorily trained teachers for
the schools at a time when education is becoming vitally
important to our national survival, or society will demand
that drastic and perhaps dangerous re-evaluations of the
entire teacher education program be made. Hopefully, we
of the teaching profession can recognize and perform our
duties without being reminded of them by persons not in the
field of education.

Note

1. Robert F. Carbone, "Big Brother Is in the Office,"
    Phi Delta Kappan, XLVII (November 1965), 34-37.

17. TRAINING TEACHERS FOR
ETHNIC MINORITY YOUTHS

Donald Hugh Smith

One of the most significant events of my life took place in Chicago during the summer of 1967. The event began officially on the Fourth of July at the East Lansing, Michigan, home of Robert L. Green, now director of Michigan State University's Center for Urban Affairs. Throughout that day and the following, six of us--educators and community developers--made final preparations for an adult literacy and job placement program funded by the Department of Health, Education, and Welfare, to be conducted on Chicago's West Side by Martin Luther King, Jr.

By the time we met with the Reverend King in Chicago the following week, the design was complete. We would teach reading, basic mathematics, and job interview skills. Dependent on their entry levels of reading and their progress, students would be placed in jobs as rapidly as possible. With eight ministers in the Lawndale and East Garfield communities providing classrooms in their churches, the eight-week program began late in July.

Yet, as this effort to rescue 400 or 500 black people on Chicago's teeming West Side was unfolding, a larger event was being superimposed which would have a lasting impact on all Americans. Early in the morning on the Sunday after our July Fourth meeting, the Detroit Rebellion began. By nightfall fire, violence, and death wracked the city. Within a few weeks, Newark was to become a second major battlefront as black people revolted in over 100 cities throughout America.

In this setting we attempted to teach reading in one of

Donald Hugh Smith, "Training Teachers for Ethnic Minority Youths," Phi Delta Kappan (January 1972), pp. 285-287. Reprinted by permission of the author and publisher.

the nation's most neglected, abused areas.   My day began
early, making the rounds of the eight churches.   It would be
difficult to describe my feelings as I drove through the city
from South to West Side, passing hundreds of "Mayor Daley's
finest" in their white battle helmets, tense, anxious, poised
to spring.   Chicago did not burn that summer, but it felt the
flames of Detroit and Newark and was terrified by the re-
membrance of its own holocausts in recent summers.

Surprising as it may seem in that electrifying environment, school attendance at those churches was very high.
Every day teen-age dropouts sat side by side with older people, poring over the materials provided by the Behavioral
Research Laboratory of California.   Some were learning to
read; others were improving their reading skills.   On several
occasions when we were ready to place some of the adults in
jobs they asked to remain in the reading program for a few
more days.   One woman said, "For the first time in my life
I'm learning to read and I want to keep on just a little while
longer. "

For a time we were euphoric--those of us who supervised the instructional program, those who taught, those who
recruited in the community, and most of all those beautiful,
tortured, poverty-stricken people who found a ray of hope in
the program.   Before long, however, the dream was crushed
and the light went out.   The serpent I call "politics before
people" reared its ugly head and killed the program.   It is
alleged that high officials in Chicago's government called the
White House.   Didn't President Johnson know that Martin
Luther King was not to have any success in Chicago?   Within
a month after its opening, King's adult literacy and jobs program closed, its grant canceled; and the director of adult
education in the U.S. Office of Education, who had authorized
the grant, was fired. People who wanted and needed desperately to read were denied the opportunity.   One could not help but
remember a similar period during the era of slavery when some
plantation owners punished those who tried to teach slaves to
read and write.   As King discovered, the right to read is political, is controversial, and--as I intend to point out--is not
the first priority in American education.

There can be no denying that the ability to read is a
skill which offers the potential for personal independence and
economic security.   There can be no denying that a man who
cannot read must be dependent upon the reading skills of
others and will be severely limited in the kind of work he can

perform. However, as critical a need as reading is, there
is something more important than the right to read.   The
right to be is more important than the right to read.

The right to be is a higher order than reading.   The
right to be is a God-given right. Reading is a skill, a faculty
of man. The right to be recognizes the inherent worth and
dignity of all human beings, of whatever color, sex, philosophy, or station in life. One can be black or white (or red,
brown, or yellow), male or female, conservative or radical;
no matter, one is still entitled to the right to exist, to live
or work wherever one's talents or interests lie.

The right to be recognizes that man is more important
than property, and that while men may own property they may
not own or control other men. If our nation honored the right
to be, it would give the same opportunity to have a job to a
poorly educated black or Puerto Rican as it gives to a poorly
educated white mountaineer or Iron Curtain refugee.

Belief in the right to be would result in a government
which would protect black school children from vicious chain-
wielding mobs that seek to deny them their right to read.   I
submit that the right to be supersedes the right to read.

Something else is more important than the right to
read.   More important than the right to read is the right to
read the truth, for the truth shall make us free.

Thomas Jefferson held the theory that if all manner of
ideas were promulgated in the marketplace of human thought
and discourse, then men would have the capacity to find the
truth.   Such a theory, of dubious validity in America's early
history, is hardly applicable to a computerized age where
control of public communication by the mass media is limited
to a very few who have their own cultural, economic, and
political interests to protect.

At no time in our history has our national ethos been
more tarnished nor our national credibility more suspect than
at the present.   It does not matter whether the truth is being
concealed or distorted by biased historians, by the mass media,
or by the President of the United States.   We are all victim-
ized by the omissions, half-truths, and out and out lies which
have characterized our national history and our present life
experience.

It should be clear that we are past the time when we can ignore the findings of a group so impeccably credentialed as President Johnson's Riot Commission. That commission told the rest of America what black people already knew: The principal cause of racial strife in America is white racism. Though the commission failed to point it out clearly, nowhere is racism more prevalent than in the public schools and public universities.

Racism permeates textbooks and teaching materials, teacher and administrative practices, and board of education policies. Fortunately, many of our beautiful young people, and even some older ones not beyond recall, are in open revolt against this system of human debasement. They are refusing to cooperate with an educational enterprise whose purpose has been historically and remains at present the preparation of an elitist few for dominant roles, and the rest for roles of service.

I know it has not been fashionable to discuss racism during the last few years, and I know that for a time those who will attempt to deal truthfully with the issues of slavery, exploitation, oppression, and repression will be branded as some form of traitor. And for a time we must pay that price. Our children and our country are both too precious to allow ourselves to be frightened by bugged telephones or secret dossiers. History records the fall of the Roman Empire in a period when its citizens had become too intimidated to discuss and debate the critical issues of the day. Instead, their public utterances were limited to neutral, nonpolitical, noncontroversial trivia. We cannot allow ourselves to become so decadent. We have to understand that coming to grips with national troubles and resolving them is our only real hope for national survival.

We who teach reading or any other subject must perceive the importance of developing in our students a burning desire to know their own personal and national truths. To teach them lies will turn them off, as it should.

Little does it matter, nor will it matter, that we live in the most literate nation in the world if those who can read continue to read of and believe in a nation where only white is right. Little will it matter if those who develop economic competence continue to exploit others in America and elsewhere. Little will it matter if the students we teach to read continue to solve their economic and political problems by killing women and children in distant lands.

        The right to read is meaningless without its antece-
dent, the right to be, and its essence, the right to read the
truth. The implications of this triumvirate--being, reading,
and reading the truth--for our schools are fairly obvious, but
the implementation is incredibly difficult in an environment
which has been so well described in the recent movies Easy
Rider and Joe, and in the horribly real dramas of Martin
Luther King, Jr., Malcolm X, Medgar Evers, and the
Kennedy brothers.

        As Easy Rider points out, America does not permit
nonconformity. Those who are free will face death if their
freedom is discovered by those who remain in conformist
chains. Joe merely underlines the issue by pointing out the
murderous hysteria of those who honestly believe they are
protecting America's values and best interests.

        Yet with full knowledge of the dangers of change we
must recognize the greater destructive potential of not owning
up to the issues. Apparently the schools and the nation will
never enjoy racial harmony and will continue to experience
violence until the schools and the nation cease to do violence
upon the minds, hearts, and bodies of its black and other
minority children.

        Where do we begin? Since behavior is a good deal
easier to change than attitudes, it would seem that the place
to start is in the materials that are being used to teach reading. The word relevance has become a cliché. It is rejected
by those who understand it to mean discarding all that has
been used in the past, and it is embraced by many who believe
it implies a whole new set of values and ideas that will usher
in a new world. I believe the concept includes parts of both,
discarding those values and practices which are dysfunctional
and adopting those new ones which promise to humanize and
civilize man.

        Specifically applied to reading, relevancy should mean
the utilization of materials and experiences which, first,
realistically and truthfully depict all races and their contributions, and second, contain content which reflects the vital
concerns and the life needs of students.

        How little understood is this simple and basic concept
is exemplified by action recently taken by a community school

board in Queens, New York. By a 5-3 vote, the board banned
Down These Mean Streets, by Piri Thomas, from its approved
reading list. As those who have read the book know, Down
These Mean Streets is the story of a Puerto Rican boy growing up in New York. He becomes a drug addict, then a
convict, and finally is rejected by his family because his skin
is black. That's where it is; that's what America's racism
did to that boy and does to us all. It is the classic story of
America's inhumanity to its own, a story that should be read
in every classroom in America, not only for its terrible truth
but also because the ultimate salvation of Piri Thomas is an
inspiration for all youths who have been abused for their
blackness.

The evidence is in: We are failing at all levels to
teach students to read. The responsibility for failure lies
with those who have controlled the schools. It lies with individual teachers who have copped out with excuses of cultural
deprivation. It lies with businesses and industries that have
permitted the public schools to fail with impunity. It lies with
governments that continue to support all manner of reading
programs designed, controlled, and operated by those who
have already failed. It lies within the churches that have
failed to teach a true religion. It lies within a national philosophy of white supremacy.

Finally, the responsibility lies within the local communities that have allowed professionals to earn excellent
salaries with no productivity. There have been exceptions
where communities have sought to control the school, but
even in most of those cases all of the energy was dissipated
in gaining control and in local power plays. These communities have rarely gotten around to the business of improving
reading and math scores. We know that poor black, Spanish-
speaking, and American Indian children can be taught to read.

Collectively, all of us--educators, business and indus-
trial leaders, clergy, government, and citizenry--must assume the responsibility for holding the schools accountable.

We should recognize, however, that to produce a new
generation of the best readers in the world will avail us
nothing if we have not also taught our children to honor and
respect themselves and others like and different from themselves. We cannot survive if we continue to turn our generations of literate Americans whose only concern is personal
profit. The improvement of reading must go hand in hand

with the elevation of the human condition and a search for truth. Our children have the right to read, but more importantly, they have the right to be.

18. PROFESSOR, IS YOUR EXPERIENCE OUTDATED?

William M. Perel and Philip D. Vairo

Professors of education are frequently held in low repute by faculty members of the academic departments because it is believed that professors of education teach students how to teach. It is an interesting observation on academic attitudes that any program which is intended to teach students how to do something is held in low repute. Thus, Phi Beta Kappa, the most prestigious honor society of academia, will not consider courses in engineering, accounting, and education because these courses are felt to be "how to do something" as opposed to being "about something." The general public also believes that the education faculty of a university devotes itself to the training of prospective teachers, and regards such training as the proper and appropriate role of the education professor within a university.

However, many professors of education are not involved at all with the training of teachers, nor do they want to be involved. Since professors of education have often been the scapegoats of the academic faculty, sometimes justly so, they have tended to play down the practical aspect of their teaching experience and focus their attention on the so-called theoretical questions of the day. As an education professor gains experience and rises in rank and seniority at his institution, there is a tendency for him to become further and further removed from the teacher training role of his institution and to become more and more involved with course work in philosophy and history of education, counseling, psychology, school administration, school social work, and so on. The above is particularly true if the professor devotes more and more of his time to graduate instruction.

William M. Perel and Philip D. Vairo, "Professor, Is Your Experience Outdated?" The Educational Forum (November 1968), pp. 39-44. Reprinted by permission of the authors and publisher.

Since our society needs teachers, and since departments, schools, and colleges of education are expected by society to prepare the needed teachers and were created for that purpose, let us accept that role. Let us accept it, not as a necessary chore, but as one of the oldest and most honored purposes of college or university education. It is very unfortunate that any university faculty member regards involvement with the training of teachers as degrading. But for a professor of education to seek to remove himself from this aspect of higher education is intolerable.

One of the major criticisms launched against teacher-training programs is that the personnel instructing the apprentice teachers have had little or no teaching experience during the past five or ten years on the level at which they are supposedly preparing teachers. To complicate matters, some of our elementary and secondary school administrators have proceeded on the naive assumption that new teachers, who are employed, know how to teach, or perhaps would learn on the job by a process of trial and error. School administrators have themselves often not actually taught for many years. However, serious as the latter problem is, it is our purpose to confine our attention here to the elementary or secondary school teaching experience of the professor of education.

The authors have found, incredible as it may seem, that professors in other disciplines who have had elementary or secondary teaching experience often seek to keep it hidden, fearing loss of status within the academic community. There is obviously no valid reason why a faculty member with experience and training in public school work should not be willing to admit to such experience and to make his training and experience available to the teacher education program. There is equally no valid reason why professors in other disciplines who are involved with training prospective teachers in subject matter should not have at least as much contact with secondary and elementary schools as could be obtained by an occasional visit to a school, perhaps to assist the education faculty in observing student teachers in his discipline. However, most academic professors would take a negative attitude to such proposals, which may in part explain why professors of education have not taken the initiative in establishing post-doctoral internships for themselves at pre-college levels. It may even explain why professors of education go so far as to differentiate themselves professionally from the public school teacher.

It must be said that the college instructor of methods
and student teaching must be a person of sufficient competence and with sufficiently recent teaching experience--in
view of the rapid changes in the profession--to be respected
by those novice teachers whom he is preparing. Certainly,
as a minimum qualification, we should demand that the professor return to full-time teaching at the grade levels at
which he prepares teachers for at least one semester every
five or six years. The professor should serve as an exchange
colleague or as a visiting teacher in a secondary or elementary
school, with his salary supplemented by his college or university, so that this exchange program would entail no financial sacrifice on the part of the professor. During this semester, the college professor should be actively involved in
observation and interclass visitations in the school at which
he is obtaining his in-service training. Teachers in the
school should have opportunities to meet with him and discuss
problems of mutual concern. He should have an opportunity
to observe demonstration lessons given by the more experienced teachers and supervisory personnel in the school. New
media and teaching innovations should be introduced to the
professor during his tenure at the school. Above all, he
should be encouraged to experiment and attempt to implement
new ideas in his daily lessons. On-the-job, in-service training
should be a real and meaningful experience for the college
professor.

It is unfortunately true that a college professor, because of his long absence from public school teaching, might
be less competent than are some of the student teachers he
is supervising. In such cases, the resentment toward and
lack of regard for the college professor, on the part of the
student, is readily understandable. Frequently, an apprentice
teacher will say, "When was the last time Dr. Jones actually
taught in a high school?" There is, indeed, no substitute
for actual classroom experience! Perhaps Dr. James B.
Conant was justified in suggesting that there is a need for a
clinical professor in education. It is not at all uncommon
for the college professor to have been away from classroom
teaching for more than fifteen years. It is easy to see why
the student teacher may find it difficult to accept advice and
criticism from the college professor, whom he cannot respect
professionally.

Yet, the very colleges and universities engaged in
educating teachers make no provisions for the college professor to return to the public school. Sabbatical leaves are

seldom, if ever, available for this purpose. Even if they
were, most professors probably would rather use their sabbaticals for purposes other than obtaining fresh experience in
pre-college teaching. Institutions not offering sabbaticals to
their staffs--and there are a large number of such institutions--
have not initiated plans, to the best of the authors' knowledge,
whereby education faculty members could return to the public
schools without substantial loss in salary. In no real sense
can a professor of education give attention to improving his
knowledge of teaching techniques at the elementary and secondary levels and broadening his horizons while he is teaching a
full load of courses at his college or university.

Before we can develop expert teachers to deal effectively with the educational problems of our day, we shall have to
expose more of our college staff to up-to-date teaching experiences in our schools. The National Education Association[1]
in a recent study pointed out three areas in which teachers
were found lacking in their preparation. These are: (1)
teaching methods (twenty-four percent); (2) classroom man-
agement routines and discipline (thirty-eight percent); (3) use
of audiovisual equipment and materials (forty-nine percent).
All three of these areas are directly related to the instruction they received by the teacher education faculty. It can be
readily recognized that the three areas mentioned above, because of their very nature, require recent teaching experience on the part of the college professor.

Many curricular changes are being implemented with
which many professors of education are not familiar. The
best known and most frequently discussed of these changes
has to do with the so-called "New Math." The Committee
on the Undergraduate Program in Mathematics (CUPM) of
the Mathematical Association of America has made an exhaus-
tive study of the mathematical training necessary for teachers
of both elementary and secondary mathematics and has published its recommendations. However, this information is
not generally known either to the education faculty or to the
mathematics faculty of most universities. Yet, typically the
teacher-training faculty is unable to give prospective teachers any instruction in or orientation to such curricula. It is
a sad situation that even teachers just out of college must rely
completely on teachers' manuals to enable them to teach these
programs. If the university faculty were more involved with
what is actually going on in the schools, they would, at the
very least, be able to provide prospective teachers with some
knowledge of what to expect.

One of the greatest problems in education today is
the education of the so-called culturally deprived or disadvantaged youth. This problem is particularly acute in urban
areas where some attempt must be made to bring young people out of the urban ghetto slums and into the mainstream of
American life.

The crisis in the preparation of teachers in this area
is due not only to inadequate resources, but also to the professor's lack of familiarity and teaching experience with the
underprivileged in our urban ghettos. Our universities and
colleges will need to redesign their teacher education programs and recruit staff who can prepare teachers in up-to-
date methods and media so that they can teach the children
of poverty.

Dr. J. C. Sitterson, Chancellor of the University of
North Carolina at Chapel Hill, reported in the Southern Education Report that teacher education graduates from his institution "are far less prepared to teach disadvantaged children than we'd like them to be or feel they should be." This
comment is typical of those from many institutions.

It is often claimed that teachers are members of the
middle class, almost by definition. Even those teachers who
grew up in slums seem to enter the middle class at the same
time they receive their teaching certificates. A great deal
that is written on this subject puts too much emphasis on
what must be done to assist the prospective teacher in obtaining knowledge and understanding of the disadvantaged.
Too little emphasis is placed upon improving the understanding of these problems upon the part of the professors of education. If teachers in the elementary and secondary schools
are middle class, surely the professors in the colleges and
universities are middle or upper middle class.

Dr. Herbert Scheuler, president of Richmond College
of the City University of New York, in a book recently published by Phi Delta Kappa, Improving Teacher Education in
the United States, says that a teacher education program for
the underprivileged and the children of poverty "cannot be
developed in an ivory tower apart and remote from the people
it is intended to serve." The fashioners and builders of
teacher education curricula must go back to the schools and
reorient themselves.

The National Council on Education for the Disadvantaged

recently singled out the attitudes of teachers as the crucial
ingredient in success or failure in teaching culturally deprived
youth. Only by actual contact with the children of the poor
can the professor readily appreciate their problems and be
able to share his experience with his own students. The professor must recognize that the children of poverty in the urban
ghettos have special problems and special needs. It is insufficient just to read about their problems in professional literature, for very frequently the authors who purport to be ex-
perts on these problems have themselves never taught in a
school serving the children of poverty.

          Professors of education, in general, have had little
experience with culturally deprived students. Thus, a cycle
is begun whereby professors with little experience in or
knowledge of the problems of teaching the culturally deprived,
teach prospective teachers, who, in turn, will not be properly
prepared to teach the children of the poor, the disadvantaged,
and the culturally deprived people of the urban slums. It is
pointless to attempt to assess blame or to heap recrimina-
tions upon the heads of professors of education or other professors. But it needs to be said over and over again that
most people in teacher education have virtually no knowledge
or experience in the problems of educating culturally disadvantaged youth. With this fact society must deal. If we are
to take decisive steps, which will break this cycle, then a
beginning must be made with the preparation of teacher education professors and with in-service education which consists
of real experience on the levels on which they are preparing
teachers.

          Much could be written about the problems of educating
culturally deprived youth. However, it is our purpose here
only to call for continuing contact between elementary and
secondary schools on the one hand and colleges of education
on the other. Cultural deprivation, curricular change, and
changes in methods of instruction are only some of the problems of the schools which those who teach teachers need to
keep constantly in mind.

          Hopefully, professors of education, if not other acade-
micians, will keep in mind that their primary function is to
prepare teachers and that they will regard this function as full
worthy of their attention and interest. Especially as a professor of education rises in rank and seniority and becomes
more and more involved with the graduate program of his institution, with all of the prestige and fringe benefits usually

associated with involvement with graduate programs, it is hoped that he will still maintain an interest and involvement with this primary function of his discipline.

Once the idea of continued involvement with the training of teachers is reestablished, surely it is only logical that the idea of periodic returns to the public school classrooms by professors of education can gain acceptance.

Note

1. Hazel Davis, "Profile of the American Public School Teacher, 1966," NEA Journal, 56:12 (May, 1967).

19. FROM STUDENT TO TEACHER

Debbie McMahan and Linda Feldman

Student teaching is a time of learning, and the learning we were exposed to in a brief eight-week period was most exciting and rewarding. As we entered the ranks of teachers, our eyes were opened to the multitude of problems of which we were to be a part.

As beginning student teachers we found the first few weeks exceptionally difficult. The schools in which we taught were located in the heart of the city. Most of the children enrolled came from homes which were culturally deprived. Putting it more emphatically, the schools were old and the neighborhoods were pockets of poverty. For us, prior experiences with children were limited mostly to younger brothers and sisters. We had no idea that so many young people came from homes so impoverished, culturally and financially. It was a useful early lesson, for we knew we would soon be responsible as teachers for working with students from socio-economic deprived circumstances.

We had been warned through methods courses and by our college supervisors, of the many pitfalls concerning our relationships with students. Before we knew it, however, we were making the very mistakes of which we had been warned. One of the first problems stemmed from our inability to withstand being a pal to the students. The transition from student to teacher was difficult. It was weeks and many experiences later before we began to recognize our new position as teachers. The result was a most significant change in the handling of students, with realization that we were their teachers, not their equals. This formally initiated us in the teaching profession. Perhaps several things which hindered an earlier transition should be mentioned at this time. First, we felt that the name "student teacher" immediately set the

Unpublished paper, included by permission of the authors.

stage for our students to recognize us as students as well, rather than as professional teachers. Secondly, age and stature, if you happen to be small, can lead to a few problems until a tone or rapport is established in the classroom-- sometimes, we were taken for students not only by the children but even by other teachers, administrators, and even parents.

Another problem we encountered was taking every action and word of the students as a personal affront. Eventually, the realization came to us that students' actions, whether in words or deeds, were directed mostly toward teachers in general, not necessarily to us personally. At first, we were not able to place student comments in the proper perspective.

The way students today act toward each other, and especially how they act toward teachers and administrators, surprised us. How different from when we were in the elementary school ourselves! Anyway, we think it is different now. Today the students appear to be so belligerent and disrespectful. But then again, we are reminded that an earlier generation made the same comments about us.

It didn't seem to matter what grade one was teaching, first or sixth; the kids were rough and discipline problems abounded. That shot for us the theory that the higher the grade one taught, the rougher the discipline. We discovered that many teachers had difficulty coping with their students-- control in some cases was at a minimum. In the schools in which we did our student teaching there was no male supervision, the principal in both cases being a woman. The only male on the staff was a teacher's aide in one of the schools, and he was resented by most of the students. These children could well have used more male images and authority at school, as some of them probably had little, if any, at home. It is possible that many of the discipline problems might have been less severe if this had been the case. As it was, order was close to impossible to maintain, and many of the teachers became discouraged and exhausted. Consequently, some of them stopped trying, thereby letting trouble constantly regenerate itself--a poor example for future teachers in training.

However, children aren't born mean and hateful, they learn these things. Environment is a great teacher, whether it be good or bad. The children learned from their surroundings--the city. Broken homes with many problems were

common. As middle class, average students, we seemed
unprepared; we had little practical experience in how to cope
with or reach these children. We lacked their experiences in
living and breathing, and they knew it. Books had not really
afforded us experience in these matters.

One of the prime prerequisites for being a teacher in
an inner city school is for the teacher to become acquainted
with the surrounding areas, the people, and the backgrounds
of the children. The teacher would then be better able to
accept the students as they are, and to utilize more patience
and understanding in the classroom solution of their problems.
One of the most difficult challenges in teaching these children,
we found, was trying to be all they needed us to be. One
had to be understanding, fair, and an honest person wearing
a variety of hats each day. We did not understand most of
their needs because we were unfamiliar with them.

School, for many of these children, was the brightest
and most pleasant place they could be during the day. The
staff within its walls needed to produce this type of atmosphere continually, and to project attitudes and personalities
relating to the students. Often the students needed a friend;
as a teacher at times it was necessary to be friend, mother,
father, referee, guidance counselor and even social worker--
a teacher was a busy person. As professional trainees it was
difficult, but necessary, to learn when to be each and when to
turn it off. If this multi-image could be effected successfully,
the children were better able to respect the teachers and us
in all roles. It was and is a very difficult position to achieve.

Outwardly, the students seemed to be growing up much
faster than a few years ago. Many of them were facing the
pressures of drugs and sex more openly. The burdens, for
some, were overbearing. Home situations, too, were not
always the best; students often had to watch younger brothers
and sisters rather than do homework, while mother was
"out" several nights a week. Many parents were unconcerned
or indifferent about their children's education. Their primary
concern, if any, seemed to be in their son's or daughter's
achievement in athletics or popularity.

Student teaching began to teach us the necessity of
accepting each child as he was. It was far beyond our power
to change them and, really, why should we? Children are
people. They can think and feel and they have a need to be
thought of as individuals. This seemed one of the best ways

to approach them--to respect them as individual human beings
with various needs and to teach them that way.

Most of the pupils in our classes were so-called "slow
learners" with short attention spans.   Very few were on grade
level in all subjects.   Some students should not even have been
in the rooms at all.   They belonged in classes for EMR (or
emotionally disturbed) children.   Many of the slower children
could not cope with the work and were simply allowed to plod
along, picking up what they could.   Many of these children
were eager to learn, but because little or no time was taken
to meet their needs, they failed to learn and fell further behind and became more frustrated as time went on.   Quickly,
we learned that our lessons had to be on a variety of levels
rather than on one grade level.   We had to at least attempt
to reach all the children and make the learning relevant to
them as well as enjoyable.   That took a great deal of time and
effort on our parts.

Many of these children will never make it to high
school, much less college.   Some of them will have to start
working early, some will wind up in penal institutions, and
some will just drop out when they reach sixteen.   Most of
them do not have the money to go on anyway, and there is little motivation in that direction from the parents.   That, however, doesn't mean that we, as teachers, should give up on
them.   These children need the very best of teachers.   Unfortunately, there are some teachers who prefer the less com-
plicated situations, with as few problems as possible.   Many
of the children suffer from the absence of successful educational experiences, and it is up to the teacher to help provide
them.   But many teachers who might be good with and for
these children end up spending three-fourths of their time
disciplining, with the result that they feel their teaching is
rarely appreciated, or often a waste; and most of them leave
for greener pastures (suburban schools).   This is unfortunate
for all involved.

Student teaching was quite an experience--a learning
situation beyond words.   We learned a great deal from the
schools we were in, from the cooperating teachers and the
pupils themselves.   In essence, we learned much about living.
We had the opportunity to see and do, and to learn from our
experiences.   We got a glimpse of what teaching was all
about, if only briefly.   Eight weeks was not nearly long
enough to give us a true picture of the profession, nor to
determine whether it was the profession for us.   Teaching

involves many problems and frustrations as well as challenges and rewards. It is full of learning every day for all
involved, an active rather than a passive vocation. All children deserve an equal chance in life, no matter what their
background and environment. That is a big responsibility
for a teacher, but that is what teaching is all about. The
human mind is a terrible thing to waste. As future teachers
who will shape these minds, student teachers need longer
and more diversified experience, in situations where they
can learn as well as teach.

   The time flew by so quickly that we no sooner realized
we had our feet on the ground than it was over. We hope we
learned far more than we gave to our classes. Next fall,
we will be on our own in schools which perhaps will be
similar, but now no longer as students, but as teachers.
We saw a great deal from a narrow periscope, but we hope
our experience will give us a broader perspective on children. Children need love and positive relationships. Discipline is important, but it should stem from love, trust, and
confidence rather than hate and punishment. We view student
teaching as just a beginning in a long, continuous training program.

20. COOPERATING TEACHERS VIEW
WORKING WITH STUDENT TEACHERS

Joyce F. Cooke and Mary D. O'Neal

Student teaching is a vital time in the training of future teachers. It is usually their first and only experience
of classroom contact during the teacher-training program.
For most students, it comes near the end of four years of
college preparation for a profession they have chosen as
their future work, and must be considered the most important, culminating aspect of this training. The experience
should be a learning one and a rewarding one. The student
teacher needs to be fully aware of teaching as a profession.
Cooperating teachers are the link to the professional world
for these trainees, and they can often make or break the
future potential of a student teacher. Being a cooperating
teacher involves a great deal of work and responsibility; it
cannot be a passive job. This article outlines certain ideas
we have found to be most useful in working with student
teachers. It is our hope that student teachers will receive
the best classroom experience, with the maximum aid to prepare them for their own classrooms and a future as successful teachers of children.

Supervising the student teacher within the inner city
schools is no easy task, but it can have many rewarding returns.

The need to facilitate the smooth adjustment of student teachers to their unfamiliar assignments by planning for
them before they arrive is very important. It is best to prepare and give the student teachers a brief written guide
which includes daily schedules, classrooms, building facilities, equipment, and so forth. When the student teacher arrives in the room, a desk or table should be ready for him
to use during his duration. In addition, desk copies of textbooks, curriculum guides, professional books and magazines

Unpublished paper, included by permission of the authors.

should be made available to help in their teaching orientation.
It is also a good idea to supply them with pencils, paper,
rubber bands, paper clips, stapler, tape dispenser, and
other things that will be needed while they are there.

It will be necessary to plan activities for the student
teacher so that she can observe principles of learning in
operation.   Such activities may include:

1.   Pupil-teacher planning
2.   Providing for individual help
3.   Handling more than one group at a time
4.   Organizing independent work periods
5.   Putting the shy child at ease during a group
     discussion
6.   Solving a discipline problem
7.   Using a variety of teaching aides for motivation
8.   Carrying children to and from other parts of the
     building
9.   Incorporating the child with a learning disability
     into the regular classroom
10.   Encouraging self-discipline
11.   Allowing for flexibility in scheduling and imple-
      menting daily lesson plans
12.   Handling classroom conditions such as lighting,
      seating and ventilation
13.   Providing attractive class displays and bulletin
      boards
14.   Creating an appropriate learning atmosphere
15.   Making assignments
16.   Evaluating pupils' progress
17.   Self-evaluation

When the student teacher arrives, begin involving her
in the classroom activities rather than giving her a seat in
the back of the room.   Begin the day by going over the aims
for the day's work.   The student teacher should be given
some samples of pupils' written work to examine.   These
will make her aware of various needs of pupils in different
subject areas, of the pupil who does above average work and
might be used in helping the slower child, or of those who
have special abilities in art and creative writing.   Also, the
student teacher may note questions she would like to ask about
certain pupils.   It is very important that she begin to learn
the pupils by name.   To help her accomplish this she could
be given a blank seating chart that she can fill in during class.
In addition, she may make notes on different pupils that she

might want to ask about.

During the first few days the student teacher should be
expected to look at texts used in class, review the lesson assignments, and study the suggestions given in the teacher's
edition. The student teacher might be asked to plan a bulletin board based on some lesson for that week; during the
planning she should discuss it with the pupils. Also during
the first week, time should be provided for the student teacher
to familiarize herself with the building facilities and to talk
with the principal, other teachers, the librarian, and other
professionals in the building.

We feel that long range planning is best. This gives
the student teacher time to order films, reserve audio-visual
equipment, plan her learning centers and bulletin boards,
and gather other materials to enhance her lessons. However,
this does not take the place of daily and weekly planning.
Weekly planning should be done one day per week. Daily conferences should be held between the student teacher and the
cooperating teacher. These may be just a few minutes, or
longer, depending on the problems or objectives; the purpose
may perhaps be just to pay a compliment to the student teacher
or to offer a suggestion for the next day. The student teacher
should always leave a copy of her lesson plan on her desk or
table, in case she is absent or one of her supervisors should
come by to inquire about her progress.

After several days of observation the student teacher
should be given full control of a small group of 10-15 pupils.
A larger group may be given, depending on the maturity of
the student teacher and how well she manages her pupils.
During the observation period the student teacher may perform such duties as overseeing independent work groups,
teaching a spelling lesson or a small reading group, reading
a story to the pupils, directing a game, grading papers, and
recording grades. This will enable her to learn and become
comfortable with the pupils.

By now the student teacher should be ready to meet
with her cooperating teacher and discuss the overview of the
program. For example, this could follow with the preparation of plans for teaching a lesson in spelling and mathematics daily. Encourage the student teacher to observe her
pupils constantly to make sure that they have been properly
motivated and are relating to her lesson.

The student teacher may gradually assume responsibility for the instruction of larger groups, depending upon the
rapport she has gained with smaller groups.   By the end of
the fourth week, the student teacher should be planning, evaluating, and executing all activities for an entire class of pupils.
This will include discussing pupils' progress with the cooperating teacher and parents in planned conferences at school or
on the telephone.   Since the success of the total school program
depends to a large degree upon the pupils' parents, it is highly
important that the student teacher systematically report pupils'
progress to parents before report cards are due.   This reporting may be by telephone, personal notes or planned conferences.   All reporting to parents should be done only after
consulting with the cooperating teacher.

During the initial stage of the student teaching period,
student teachers should be encouraged to keep a log folder
on their pupils.   This should include items that may be used
during the conferences or general evaluation of pupils.

Ask any seasoned inner city teacher what her biggest
problem is today and she will probably say, discipline.   It is
true that a teacher cannot teach well when the pupils are inat-
tentive or distracted by other pupils or objects.   If getting
the pupils' attention is a major problem for the experienced
teacher, is it not true that discipline will prove to be an even
bigger problem for the student teacher in many cases?   What
then should the student teacher do?   First, let's get a good
working definition of discipline; let's look at what discipline
is, rather than what it isn't.   We are convinced that good
discipline is consistent, sometimes quiet, honest, fair, and
sometimes forceful.   The best disciplinary cure is to see that
the student teacher keeps the pupils actively involved in enjoyable and constructive learning activities.   Pupils who are
enjoying learning are very seldom disciplinary problems.

The cooperating teacher should never interrupt when
the student teacher is disciplining a pupil.   If she feels that
justice has not been done, she should discuss this privately
with the student teacher and work out some possible solution.
Student teacher and cooperating teacher should always be together in the final disciplinary decisions.

The student teacher, after appropriate preparation,
should be left alone with the class so that the pupils will fully
realize that they are to respect her as a teacher.   However,
the student teacher should know where to find the teacher in

case she needs her. She could be told before class begins that the cooperating teacher will leave the room for awhile, or the cooperating teacher could leave a note telling where she can be found. The cooperating teacher should not expect a student teacher to use the same disciplinary methods that she uses but should discuss her ideas of discipline with the student teacher and then let her develop her own measures. No matter what the situation is, the student teacher should be encouraged always to display self-control.

Helpful hints for the cooperating teacher:

1. Begin with a positive attitude.

2. Look for the good teaching points and help correct the bad ones.

3. Encourage creativity in your student. (Students love this element in a teacher.)

4. Make use of the many useful ideas which may be shared by your student teacher. Students fresh from the University usually have a wealth of new ideas which, if accepted, will enhance the total learning program.

5. Remember that your role is only to serve as a guide or advisor.

6. Set a workable relaxed atmosphere during the initial period. Pupils work better in a comfortable relaxed surrounding, and so does the student teacher. See that this atmosphere is maintained throughout the student teaching period.

7. Give criticism in a positive and constructive manner.

8. Leave the student teacher alone with the class at times, to show that you have confidence in her.

9. Include the student teacher in conferences and conversations with parents and introduce her to all visitors.

10. Help the student teacher to have a feeling of security by respecting her ideas and accepting her as another teacher.

11.   Show appreciation for any extra work that she might do.

12.   Make sure the student teacher understands what assistance is expected of her in sharing room duties.

13.   Be consistent in all areas.

14.   Never interrupt the student while she is teaching.

15.   Don't wait until the last minute to provide activities and assignments for the student teacher.

16.   Refrain from complaining to the student teacher about other members of the faculty, work loads, or other teaching responsibilities.

Helpful hints for the student teacher:

1.   Look to the cooperating teacher as an advisor, not a supplier of all the ideas.

2.   Confer with your cooperating teacher on any point that may be confusing you.   She loves to feel needed.

3.   Always confer with your cooperating teacher before seeking the advice of a fellow teacher.

4.   Do not become pals with the pupils before they have had a chance to learn to respect you as their immediate supervisor.

5.   Don't let love of pupils interfere with what you've learned about pupils' progress.

6.   Individualize your assignments as much as possible. What is needed for John may not be needed for Mary.

7.   Be genuinely interested in the pupils' learning.   Pupils seem to enjoy best the teachers who show that they are interested in them.

8.   Be resourceful, punctual, and enthusiastic.

9.   Be consistent in all areas.

10.   Strive to improve yourself by being open-minded and enjoy your teaching.

Cooperating teachers have to be good. They have to be ready and willing to contribute their time and efforts to work fully with their student teachers. They are images which may follow and influence their student teachers for years to come. The rewards can be most worthwhile if we have really put our efforts into the job. Yes, it is a responsibility; one that we hope all who are involved or committed to will truly work towards--the preparation of good teachers for tomorrow's schools. It would be foolish to conclude that the present system of training teachers is acceptable. A great deal needs to be changed; but within the present operating mode, we believe that the suggestions and comments offered simply make good sense. In the decade ahead, pretty good teachers will not suffice.

21. WANTED: 20,000 MALE
FIRST-GRADE SCHOOL TEACHERS

Philip D. Vairo

During the last decade there have been many innovative programs reported. So far, there have been few reports in the professional literature on the success of recruiting male teachers for the elementary school, especially for the first grade--an arrangement which the author believes offers distinct advantages, especially for pupils.

Over the last several years the author has had the opportunity to discuss this problem with over two hundred elementary school principals and teachers from New York and North Carolina. In all instances, it was found that they could not recall a male teacher instructing at the primary level, grades one through three. In a few cases it was reported that male teachers have served on the staff at the fifth- and sixth-grade levels. However, after a relatively short tenure, the male teacher moved on to administrative positions or to secondary schools.

Social Change and the Family

The rapid social and cultural change which is taking place in urbanized industralized communities complicates the first-grader's adjustment at home and in the neighborhood and, hence, affects his psycho-social security as well as his ability to learn. That segmented character of urban life, which has become the dominant mode in American society, has resulted in the ascendancy of secondary over primary relationships, thus weakening the primary group structure, the family, and its controls. With urbanization has come social disorgani-

Philip D. Vairo, "Wanted: 20,000 Male First-Grade School Teachers," Education (February-March 1969), pp. 222-224. Reprinted by permission of the author and publisher.

zation, insecurity, and family disintegration. The positive
male image is rapidly disappearing from the American scene.

In the everyday family lives of our economically deprived citizens, in particular the Mexican, the Black, and the
Puerto Rican, the wife in many instances receives a more
lucrative job than her husband. The husband's identity as
breadwinner of the household, of course, is threatened. Thus,
the young child is vulnerable to identity diffusion in his cultural environment and his concepts of behavior appropriate to
the sexes differs from the values and expectations of the
community. His contact with the female teacher in the primary grades only reinforces his home experiences. It is
usually not until the child reaches junior high school, and in
some communities senior high school, that he is taught by a
male teacher. In many instances, a traumatic crisis may
arise over this new experience.

At this point let us not forget the children of broken
families, born out of wedlock, and whose fathers are deceased.
The child without a father figure in the home will be deprived
of male leadership and direction in his early formative years.
These youngsters need to have contact with both sexes in
order to learn to alternate their modes of behavior in response to the sexes.

The male teacher can influence the child's feelings
about learning by his own attitude and example. He can help
the child view attainment of knowledge and school success as
worthy activities. The security derived from the male teacher
can well be a basic ingredient of academic learning for many
culturally deprived fatherless first-graders. The male's central importance in the classroom will be a visible sign to the
child of the trustworthy and representative role he will play in
the grown-up world--a world where he will be expected to
take his place like all other children who have had the benefit
of male exposure and companionship.

Identity Association and the Learning Process

It is generally recognized that learning problems are
more common among boys than among girls, especially in
reading. The latency years are a very important period when
the child develops an identity. A young boy, whose primary
adult contacts may consist solely of his mother and his female
first-grade teacher, may develop a faulty identification with the

male sex and his father in particular. In essence, a poor masculine identification with the male sex and a distorted self-image may develop during those early formative years. Reading, school success, and even the teaching profession itself, in the eyes of the first-grader, may be equated with femininity.

By the age of six a boy usually affiliates with his father. However, if he has no model to imitate, perhaps he may learn to avoid aggression and self-assertion and so find a masculine role awkward when circumstances place him in it. A balanced elementary faculty needs a variety of personalities as well as men on its staff. [1]

The author believes that one of the reasons for the rise in adolescent delinquency during the last two decades can be traced as far back as the first grade where the kind of men boys should model themselves after have been non-existent. As these youngsters approach the early adolescent period they may pattern their behavior and mode of thinking after criminals, ball players, television characters, and Hollywood entertainers. The lower grades need to provide opportunity for our students to express their masculine qualities. Male teachers are needed who can provide suitable activities in order to challenge a boy's physical aptitude as well as his mental outlook. A boy needs to have a masculine idol--if he does not find one in school, he will turn to the streets, to the local gang, to the dope addict, or to the poolhall.

Recruiting Male Teachers

Here is one of the most critical problems the elementary schools face: the prospective male teacher wants no part of teaching first-graders. Conversely, the author was horrified to learn that there is a belief in educational quarters that female teachers are biologically superior for this role. This attitude is as archaic as the horse and buggy on Madison Avenue.

In a sense, teacher education in this country is at a crossroad; when and how shall we attract men to teach in the grades, especially at the primary level? There has been much progress in the last decade in teaching techniques and media and there is the probability of much more in the decade ahead. However, it appears that there is an urgent need to make

personnel changes in our schools in order to promote the
healthy growth of our children. We will have passed up indeed an almost incredible opportunity if we stand still on
this issue.

The prestige of the elementary school must be raised,
and its image altered in professional circles, if it is to attract
qualified men. There is need for a concerted effort on the
part of Schools of Education, placement officers, school
boards, and shool administrators to encourage prospective
male candidates to teach in the elementary school. Such in-
centives as equal teaching loads with secondary schools, free
preparation periods, and duty-free lunch hours merit serious
consideration.   The plain fact is that men will hesitate to
teach in the lower grades unless the above-cited suggestions
are implemented, and the cultural stigma that is attached to
teaching younger children is erased. The teacher supply and
demand, of course, will play an important role in recruitment and teacher preparation.

Conclusion

It is true that the teaching profession has been largely
preoccupied with establishing appropriate techniques and service programs, but it has never closely examined the results
of the femininity which dominates our elementary schools.
There is genuine need for educators to inquire into the role
of ego identity. It is generally agreed that the process of
identity formation does not begin in adolescence. Ego identity
actually evolves during the period of infancy and sexual identity
is usually established long before adolescence. For much too
long, we have set our sights at the material surroundings of
the classroom; the time has come for us to broaden them.
If and as we do, we shall witness the breakthrough in elementary education too long coming.

Note

1. Lee J. Cronbach, Educational Psychology (New York,
        Harcourt, Brace & Company, Inc., 1954), pp. 316-
        318.

DEAR TEACHER

Connie Shattuck

I want your love, your
understanding, and your
guidance.

I want you to be a
good model because
I will practice what
I hear and see you do.
I will pattern my life
after yours.

I will watch you every day
and some days I
may pretend I am
you.

Please discipline me
but be strict and fair.

If you will try hard
to be a good, understanding,
patient, hardworking
and concerned individual,
then maybe I will be one
in the coming days of
my life.

Unpublished poem, included by permission of the author.

CONTRIBUTORS

ADAMS, ANNE H., Associate Professor of Education, Duke University.

BAZELI, FRANK P., Associate Professor of Education, Northern Illinois University.

BERLIN, BARNEY, Chairman, Department of Curriculum and Instruction, Loyola University, Chicago.

COOKE, JOYCE F., Teacher, Chattanooga City Schools.

DEIULIO, ANTHONY M., Professor of Education, State University College, Fredonia, New York.

FELDMAN, LINDA, University of Tennessee at Chattanooga Student Teacher (Ridgedale Elementary School), Spring 1973; Chattanooga City Schools.

GOOD, RONALD G., Associate Professor of Science Education, Florida State University.

JOHNSON, KENNETH R., Associate Professor of Education and Ethnic Studies, University of California at Berkeley.

KOREY, RUTH, Associate Professor of Education, Fordham University.

KRAJEWSKI, ROBERT J., Assistant Professor of Education, The University of Tennessee at Chattanooga.

LEEP, ALBERT G., Associate Professor of Education, Ohio University.

McMAHAN, DEBBIE, University of Tennessee at Chattanooga Student Teacher (Barger Elementary School), Spring 1973; Chattanooga City Schools.

MATCZYNSKI, THOMAS J., Associate Professor of Education,

Wright State University.

O'NEAL, MARY D., Teacher, Chattanooga City Schools.

PEREL, WILLIAM M., Chairman, Department of Mathematics, Wichita State University.

PRESTON, THOMAS R., Chairman, Department of English, University of Wyoming.

RICHMOND, BERT O., Associate Professor of Education, University of Georgia.

SHATTUCK, CONNIE, University of Tennessee at Chattanooga Student Teacher (Barger Elementary School), Spring 1973; Chattanooga City Schools.

SHUMAN, R. BAIRD, Professor of Education, Duke University.

SIMONS, HERBERT D., Assistant Professor of Education, University of California at Berkeley.

SMITH, DONALD HUGH, Professor of Education and Director of Educational Development at Bernard M. Baruch College, City University of New York.

SUBLETT, HENRY L., Jr., Associate Professor of Education, Duke University.

VAIRO, PHILIP D., Dean, School of Education, California State University, Los Angeles.

VINCI, THOMAS, Professor of Education, Fordham University.

YOUNG, JAMES M., Sixth-grade Teacher and Career Education Program Director, Bemus Point Central School System, Bemus Point, New York.

INDEX

Abilities, 46
Achievement, 64, 67, 128
Accountability, 107-113
Accountability model, 111-
113
Adams, Anne H. , 28
Administrator,
role of, 7
Aides 160
technological, 6-12
Alienation, 128
Anderson, William, 46, 48
Arbuthnot, May Hill, 19
Art, 101, 105
Assignments, 95-106, 123-
130
Attention, 7
Attention span, 30, 121, 157
Attitude
parent, 30
pupil, 24, 56, 136
student, 136
Awareness
ecological, 95-106

Background
pupil, 1, 6, 46, 48, 62, 65,
115, 117, 124, 156, 158
Bandura, 5
Barro, Stephan, 108-110
Bazeli, Frank P. , 1
Behavioral Research Lab. ,
California, 141
Benefits
oral reading, 13-27

Berlin, Barney, 107
Betts, Emmett Albert, 13,
17
Black children, 87-94
Black Culture, 87-89
Black dialect, 89-93
Bloom, Benjamin, 2
Bordan, Diane, 23
Bruner, Jerome, 1, 81
Bulletin board, 161

Carbone, Robert F. , 135
Career education, 73-78
Child rejection, 32
Children
black, 87-94
criticism of, 32-33
cruelty to, 33
disadvantaged, 6, 28-38,
61-70, 115-122, 150,
152
ghetto, 123-130
handicapped, 32, 36
inner-city, 1-2, 6, 45
mentally retarded, 34
minority, 140-146
over protected, 35
self concept, 39, 62, 67,
77, 116-119, 121, 128-
129, 167
underprivileged, 28
Choral reading, 19, 26
Cities
Chicago, 140, 141
Detroit, 140, 141

173